# AI on The Job

Andreas Moring

# AI on The Job

## Guide to Successful Human-Machine Collaboration

Springer

Andreas Moring
International School of Management (ISM)
Hamburg, Hamburg, Germany

This book is a translation of the original German edition „KI im Job " by Moring, Andreas, published by Springer-Verlag GmbH Germany in 2021. The translation was done with the help of artificial intelligence (machine translation by the service DeepL.com). A subsequent human revision was done primarily in terms of content, so that the book will read stylistically differently from a conventional translation. Springer Nature works continuously to further the development of tools for the production of books and on the related technologies to support the authors.

ISBN 978-3-662-64004-3 ISBN 978-3-662-64005-0 (eBook)
https://doi.org/10.1007/978-3-662-64005-0



This Springer imprint is published by the registered company Springer-Verlag GmbH, DE part of Springer Nature.
The registered company address is: Heidelberger Platz 3, 14197 Berlin, Germany

# Foreword

We are moving to the next stage of the industrial revolution with artificial intelligence. The fourth industrial revolution is already characterized by increasing digitalization, digital networking, and advancing automation, especially in industry. Companies are in the midst of their own digital transformation, which is also linked to a cultural change in values in the world of work. In this context, the individual experience and behavior of people in the work context is increasingly coming to the fore. In terms of empowerment, the aim is to support and enable employees with their skills and potential in order to be able to act in a motivated manner, without fears and with the necessary resources in the digital working world, in which artificial intelligence plays an increasing role.

This becomes even more important when we think of the increasing importance of human-machine interaction with artificial intelligences. This is exactly what this book deals with. It explores the question of how the design of new technologies and applications of artificial intelligence should look so that the cooperation between humans and machines is not only effective and productive but can also take place in a self-determined manner and with appropriate acceptance.

The book provides an overview of human-machine interaction in the context of developments in artificial intelligence. Furthermore, relevant theories such as the technology acceptance model, the self-determination theory, and the job demands-resources model are described and discussed in their current relevance. The subsequent study, which consists of qualitative interviews and a quantitative survey, sheds light on the one hand on the requirements for future professional activities in collaboration with artificial intelligence and on the other hand identifies resources that are of particular importance for an implementation of AI technologies. The great added value of the book lies in the fact that, on the basis of the theoretical discussion and empirical analysis, a practice-oriented guideline for AI implementation in companies is derived.

Thus, as a reader, you will gain a theoretical insight into relevant theories in the context of collaboration between humans and artificial intelligence, founded on practical research and application-oriented guidelines. In all of this, the human being is the focus of the digital working world, which is increasingly shaped by AI.

I hope you will gain a lot of knowledge and inspiration from reading this book and that you will enjoy implementing it in your own business practice.

I would like to congratulate Andreas Moring on the publication and wish him an extensive and intensive reception of the book.

Organization designer, coach, and author.

**Melanie Hasenbein**
Munich, Germany
October 2020

# Contents

# Introduction

Contents




A. Moring, *AI on The Job*,
https://doi.org/10.1007/978-3-662-64005-0_1

1

Artificial intelligence will change businesses, organizations, the way we work, and the entire economy and society. These are big predictions. Of course, no one can predict the future with complete accuracy. Nevertheless, the major lines of development are clear and the one described in the first sentence is one of them. Missing from the first sentence, however, is something crucial: People. New technologies can be as powerful and revolutionary as they are. They will only prevail if people, if we like to use them and work and interact with them productively. But for this to happen, the circumstances have to be right and the right leadership is essential. In recent years, a great deal has been researched and written on the topic of working environments and digitalization. However, the special and very unique characteristics of artificial intelligence have not yet been studied in depth with this focus and goal. This is exactly what this book is about.

## 1.1 Question and Objective

In the past 2–3 years, the topic of "artificial intelligence"has experienced a steady increase in attention and importance. This applies both to the economic and entrepreneurial perspective and equally to the social and political perspective. The governments of the major industrial and economic powers are competing to outdo each other in emphasizing the importance of AI for the future of their respective economies. China and the US, in particular, are not content with just words, but are investing heavily in the development of a wide range of AI technologies on a large scale. Therefore, the generally accepted opinion in the media, politics and science is that these two economic areas will determine this strategic future field. However, other countries such as Canada, Israel and France are also successfully positioning themselves as growing and attractive AI locations on a global scale. Germany has also adopted a national AI strategy, but has significantly reduced its funding compared to its original plans. Nevertheless, Germany is also one of the major players in business and research.

Of course, these developments do not pass society and the public by without leaving a trace. Thus, the future of the economy and society is increasingly discussed through the AI revolution. As is almost always the case, opinions differ greatly. While one side tends to see in the increased use of AI technologies an opportunity to achieve new levels of efficiency and at the same time also sustainability and performance in many dimensions, the other side fears in the worst case the subjugation of humanity under machines and autonomous systems or even a superintelligence. All those who are at least fundamentally familiar with AI technologies are sceptical about such extreme scenarios because they interpret more into the technologies than they are capable of or what they have been developed for. However, these discussions show that the question of the distribution of power and tasks between humans and (intelligent) machines and the idea of future cooperation between humans and artificial intelligence touches on and emotionalizes fundamental convictions and values. And that is precisely what this book is about.

After the initial hype, the economic view of AI technologies has now also become quite sober and pragmatic. AI is seen as a new means of optimizing a wide variety of tasks and processes and as a way of automating entire value creation processes at various levels. Contributing to this pragmatic view is the fact that word has now spread that artificial intelligence is not a recent invention of digitalization. The beginnings of AI development date back to the 1950s, with several subsequent advances and setbacks, the so-called "AI winters", over the past decades. What has now helped Artificial Intelligence, or more precisely Machine Learning, to blossom again and achieve a breakthrough of sorts in recent years is, on the one hand, the greatly increased performance of today's computers and their capacities and processors, and on the other hand, the ever-growing mass of data that is available. Both are absolutely necessary for the (further) development of AI technologies and their application in practice. Why this is so is explained in the chapter on AI technologies in this book.

#### ■ The Fifth Stage of the Industrial Revolution

With the triumph of artificial intelligence, companies, economies and societies are entering a new stage of the industrial revolution. The economy and society are changing rapidly. We know that. But the really interesting question is: Where to? We don't know the exact answer either. And it doesn't matter. Because no one can know. Or did anyone really know at the time of the invention of electricity what kind of devices, companies, products and business models it would make possible? At the time of the invention of the internet protocol, did anyone foresee or even know what would come of it 10, 20 or 30 years later? So whoever claims today, whether person or company, to already know the possibilities, concrete potentials and best strategies of the future, should perhaps rather sit in a tent at the fair in front of a crystal ball and a game of cards. We can, however, do something different. Namely: Describe the current situation and derive from it conclusions, approaches and methods to find the best way into the future. ... and thereby help to shape this future ourselves. The writer and philosopher André Malraux already knew that "if you want to read the future, you have to leaf through the past".

**Definition**

The fifth stage of industrial evolution

In economic terms, we are on the threshold of the fifth stage of development in the economy and the world of work:

1. Industrial mechanization,
2. Electrification,
3. Mobilization (cars, planes, etc.),
4. Digitization,
5. Autonomization of machines and systems and a new kind of cooperation between man and machine

There is a significant "missing link" for this fifth stage. Namely, the answer to the question of how this symbiotic or hybrid activity and work of humans and intelligent machines with each other can and should look, and in such a way that each of the two parties does and uses what it does best. Humans, for example, are very good at developing, training, and managing various AI applications. This is how humans make it possible for machines and systems to act as true collaborative partners. Machines and systems, on the other hand, can help humans grow beyond themselves and their natural abilities, for example, when it comes to capturing, calculating, and outputting almost unfathomable amounts of information and data from billions of sources in real time. Machines and systems expand human capabilities into new dimensions. Or even to the fifth level of our working and living environment.

> The question of this thesis is therefore: How can the implementation and use of artificial intelligence technologies and applications be designed in such a way that it promotes effective and productive human-machine collaboration?

Technical aspects play a role in addressing and answering this question, as do previous findings on human-machine and human-computer interaction. At the same time, the focus is also on theories and models of motivation and performance research. After all, only motivated and open-minded people can realize the theoretical potential of AI-based technologies in everyday workflows, processes and companies. Artificial intelligence will automate many processes and perform many tasks autonomously. However, the interface with humans and cooperation with humans will always remain. Only differently than before...

#### Relevance of the Question

This raises a key question for the success of organizations in the "AI age". The most recent confirmation of this thesis is the study published in mid-2020 by the Münchner Kreis and the Bertelsmann Stiftung under the title "Leben, Arbeit, Bildung 2035 + " (Münchner Kreis e. V., Bertelsmann Stiftung (eds.) Leben, Arbeit, Bildung 2035 + 2020). In response to the question "How big will the influence of AI be on the following areas in the next 10 to 15 years?", 86% of respondents cited "work", behind mobility (92%) and ahead of health (81%), media (79%) or education (61%). It is known and proven from various disciplines of scientific research and entrepreneurial practice that in the so-called human-machine interaction, the willingness and acceptance of people towards (new) technical applications are the most important key to success and productivity in application and cooperation. In other words, the potential of artificial intelligence can only be realized in organizations if the people in the organization are also involved and motivated. When it comes to technical issues and application examples or implementation examples at the process level, the research and experience situation is quite good and extensive. For the interface between humans and intelligent machines or intelligent systems, however, the situation is much slimmer. One could certainly say that the human factor has been rather overlooked and certainly underestimated so far. However, there is a lot of evidence and examples that the "right" cooperation and division of tasks between the machine or system and the human being is the decisive starting point for achieving maximum performance and exceeding previous limits.

In the former year, 1997, the world chess champion Garry Kasparov lost for the first time against the then IBM supercomputer Deep Blue, a kind of precursor of today's AI system Watson. Had humans once again had a domain snatched away from them by "intelligent machines" that no one had previously imagined or wanted to happen? In 2005, things changed. The main actors in the next chapter of the story of man and machine: Garry Kasparov and computers. Unlike in 1997, however, this time it wasn't a question of pitting humans against computers. In this new "freestyle" tournament, teams can include any combination of human and digital players. With amazing results. "The teams of humans and machines dominated even the strongest computer. The chess machine Hydra, a chess-specific supercomputer from Deep Blue, was no match for a strong human player using a relatively weak laptop. The combination of human strategic leadership and the tactical acumen of a computer was overwhelming. The surprise came at the end of the event. The winner turned out to be not a grandmaster with a state-of-the-art PC, but a couple of American amateur chess players using three computers simultaneously. Their ability to use and "coach" their computers to check positions very extensively very successfully countered the superior chess knowledge of their grandmaster opponents and also the greater computer power of other participants. Weak man + machine + better method was superior to a strong computer alone, and more remarkably, they were also better than a strong man + machine + weaker method." (Garry Kasparov: The Chess Master and the Computer, Kasparov 2010).

**■ Man + Machine = Exponential Increase**

What does that mean? Humans and machines do not approach the same task in the same way. If that were the case, if computers and algorithms mimicked human behavior, they would have long since overtaken humans with their superior optimization capabilities. But that hasn't happened. Nor is it foreseeable that it would in the future. Machines are good at performing a task particularly well, for which they or their (neuronal) networks have been trained. Instead, we recognize that humans can still realize huge potential when playing chess at the highest level, if humans can compete with machines rather than against them. What is true for complex tasks like chess is without question also true for complex and demanding tasks in modern companies and organizations. It is therefore important to find the right way in the interaction of man and machine in companies and processes in order to be able to exploit the existing potential.

Computers are perfect at optimizing given tasks and procedures. This can even go so far as to "over-optimize" results. We have seen and experienced this in the course of digitization and machinization in virtually all industries and contexts over the past decades, be it in advertising marketing, e-commerce, logistics or industrial manufacturing. But when we look at examples of activities we haven't seen from computers until now, the idea of a "new idea" keeps popping up there. We have never seen a truly creative machine, or an entrepreneurial one, or an innovative one. Even if there are "poems" created by machines or "paintings" fabricated by self-learning systems: All are ultimately reproductions of learned patterns, merely spit out here in a mathematically optimized form by computers. No machine can decide on its own what it wants to write another poem about or what kind of picture it will paint next.

Ideation in its many manifestations is nowadays an area in which humans have an advantage over machines. Humans can question, perceive intuitively, seek new solutions on their own initiative, formulate hypotheses. Machines can only give answers to questions that humans give them. That's already an incredible amount. Especially when machines are now able to find their own way to the answer. But the interesting new questions must always come from humans. Even Voltaire knew - long before AI even existed - that what matters is this: "Judge men by their questions rather than by their answers."

The high importance of human emotion and motivation is also clearly proven in the area of so-called change management. Only if people also accept changes emotionally and if they are even motivated in the best case, then change processes in companies can also be implemented successfully and with recognizable results. The introduction of technologically new processes, such as AI-based systems and applications, are such change processes. Since AI will change not only procedures and processes but also tasks, domains and hierarchies, this is also about change management at a higher level. If this is to succeed, it is critical to know which factors and circumstances can promote the will to change and motivation among employees. This then has an impact on the type of management and leadership, not only in the change process itself, but also beyond. It can be assumed that leadership in the AI age will have to be understood and defined differently, because communication and the management of employees will also have to adapt to changes in task and job profiles. In addition, it will no longer only be necessary to "lead" people, but also systems that could act partially autonomously, make their own decisions and in turn trigger further processes without requiring human approval or an explicit order from a "superior".

## 1.2 Current State of Research

There are a large number of differently focused sources on the technologies and applications in the field of artificial intelligence. For example, in the last 2–3 years alone, a large number of publications can be found that deal with the functioning and practical development and use of AI technologies. The bandwidth here ranges from general publications on Artificial Intelligence (cf. Ertel 2018; Lämmel and Cleve 2020; Buxmann and Schmidt 2019) and Data Science (Cf. among others: Igual and Segui 2017; Oettinger 2018; VanderPlas 2017) to more specific and focused works on individual areas such as Machine Learning, Deep Learning, Natural Language Processing, Image Recognition, Predictive Analytics and more (Cf. among others: Aggarwal 2018; Goodfellow and Bengio 2019; Doherty et al. 2016).

In addition, studies and white papers on the topic of artificial intelligence are regularly published by a wide variety of authors. These include publications on current trends and developments, for example by Harvard or Stanford University or the University of Oxford (cf. Stanford University 2020; University of Oxford et al. 2018), as well as publications in German-speaking countries by the Fraunhofer Institute or the Learning Systems Platform (e.g.: Fraunhofer Institute 2018; Plattform Lernende Systeme 2020a, b). At the same time, various companies and think tanks regularly issue new publications on different aspects of the development and use of artificial intelligence (e.g.: Deloitte 2020; McKinsey Global Institute 2017).

The discipline of human-machine and human-computer interaction has not really ventured into the topic of artificial intelligence. Although new publications have appeared in recent years that also deal with AI, they do not focus on it. Liggieri and Müller provide the most up-to-date and comprehensive overview of human-machine interaction in their Handbook on Human-Machine Interaction, published in 2020 (Liggieri and Müller 2019). Likewise, the publication by Butz and Krüger can be considered the current standard work on human-machine interaction (Butz and Krüger 2017). However, artificial intelligence does not play a role here. In their work published in 2020, Bartneck et al. address the current state of human-robot interaction and illuminate and analyze the topic from various perspectives such as design, spatial interaction, verbal and nonverbal interaction, and also address the role of emotions and the motivational effects in the cooperation of humans and human-like machines (Bartneck et al. 2020).

The situation is similar with research on motivation theories. Here, too, there are various standard models and standard works, some of which are several decades old - but which have proven themselves over the sometimes long period of time in science and practice. However, explicit research on the relationship between AI and motivation is not available. In this respect, some of these models and publications are used in this research and adapted to the research question of the thesis and in the analysis. However, this is not a disadvantage or a weakness, as the models such as the technology acceptance model or the jobs demands-resources model are per se general models and theories that are deliberately kept open for different possible technologies and circumstances.

Relatively many sources and publications can be found for the area of theoretical and practical AI implementation. In addition to studies and white papers by individual companies or consultancies, more comprehensive publications can also be found. For example, the publications by Daugherty and Wilson (Daugherty and Wilson 2018) or by Agrawal, Gans and Goldfarb (Agrawal et al. 2018) are worth mentioning here. In mid-2020, the Learning Systems Platform in Germany also issued a white paper that explicitly focuses on human-machine cooperation with artificial intelligence and formulates rules for implementation (Plattform Lernende Systeme 2020a). Prior to this, the High Level Expert Group on Artificial Intelligence of the European Commission had already published its "Ethics Guidelines for trustworthy AI" in 2019 (Independent High Level Expert Group on Artificial Intelligence 2019), which are also intended to serve as a guide and orientation for the practical implementation of artificial intelligence and the cooperation between humans and machines.

When it comes to changing work environments and new principles of leadership and employee motivation, the research and source material is again very extensive and diverse in terms of topics and focal points. The so-called "New Work" philosophy has been very successful in science and practice for several years (e.g. Brommer et al. 2020). In practice, however, it is often questionable whether everything that is done under the label "New Work" is really so new and different and whether it has anything to do with the actual philosophy. However, this is no different with other hypes and fads... In 2019, Cornelia Gerdenitsch and Christian Korunka dealt with the digital transformation of the working world. With their work, the authors provide an overview of the changes in the world of work triggered by digitalization. Based on psychological theories and empirical results, the aim is to provide a deeper understanding of the consequences of a digital transformation in terms of experience and behavior for working people, various workplace concepts are derived, and the authors also shed light on human-machine interaction in terms of communication and coordination with intelligent machines and robots and the resulting requirements and challenges for management (Gerdenitsch and Korunka 2019). A more detailed focus on humans in the digital world of work is provided by Hasenbein's 2020 study, which examines the impact of digitalization on humans in today's working and organizational world and addresses the aspects of leadership competencies in the digital age, changes and developments in teamwork, digital learning formats, and digital balance and ethics (Hasenbein 2020). In this context, the changing human-machine cooperation plays an important role, especially when it comes to "intelligent" machines, as these are associated with fears and at the same time also with hopes, and are even overloaded in some cases.

Geramanis and Hutmacher 2018 also dealt extensively with new worlds of work by asking about the various dimensions and definitions of identity and thus also motivation in new worlds of work and analysing the topic from various perspectives of scientific disciplines (Geramanis and Hutmacher 2018). In 2020, the two aforementioned authors deepened the topic even further in relation to self-organization and the transfer of responsibility of employees in companies (Geramanis and Hutmacher 2020; on the field of "leadership" see also: Geramanis and Hermann 2016). Wörwag and Cloots also recently investigated new aspects of leadership and the (self-)organization and motivation of employees in digital work environments (Wörwag and Cloots 2020). Weber and Manzeschke have dealt with ethical issues in (autonomous) assistance systems and developed their own model for this (Manzeschke 2015). Although there is a large body of work on new leadership and motivation concepts in connection with digital transformation, a research gap can be identified when it comes to employee motivation in connection with artificial intelligence.

## 1.3 Structure of the Book

The course of the following investigation is based on the topics already mentioned in the overview of the current state of research. First, an overview of the state of the art and the most important aspects and questions of human-machine and human-computer interaction is given in the following ► Chap. 2. Since this thesis deals with a new aspect, namely that of artificial intelligence and autonomous systems, of human-machine interaction, such an overview is obligatory.

Also necessary and self-evident is an overview of the most important technologies and functionalities of artificial intelligence, which is given in ► Chap. 3. In this chapter, the history of the development of AI will not be discussed further, as this has already been sufficiently presented in other publications. Rather, the focus is on the technical and logical details of the development and use of AI disciplines such as Machine Learning, Deep Learning and on basic concepts such as Neural Networks or Recurrent Neural Networks. Even though these are advanced and complex principles and concepts, they are still quite understandable and comprehensible to "non-programmers" and "non-data scientists". Without these technical explanations and their understanding, the further analyses and evaluations of human-AI collaboration in the last third of the book would be difficult or impossible for readers to comprehend.

► Chapter 4 offers a description of the most important theories of technical adaptation. The focus here is placed on the technology acceptance model, as this model is the most appropriate for the research question of the thesis. This is followed in ► Chap. 5 by an overview of basic concepts in motivation research. This deals with achievement motivation, connection motivation and power motivation, which can be explained differently and manifest themselves differently. At the end of the study, these three basic principles are referred to again and adapted to human-machine cooperation with AI-based systems.

► Chapter 6 presents the self determination theory, which builds on the three basic motives of motivation named and described in the previous chapter. Since the question of self-determination and control must clearly play a role in dealing with (partially) autonomous systems and applications, the corresponding theoretical models and findings must also be described here and placed in the context of the thesis question.

The following ► Chapter 7 provides a detailed description of the jobs demands-resources model. This model considers the relationship between the demands of the job on the employee (Demands) in relation to the means and circumstances available to the employee to perform the job (Resources). The relationship between demands and resources has proven and clearly identifiable effects on employee motivation and performance. Since the use and implementation of AI-based systems and tools must change the requirements for employees to cooperate with these systems, it is a critical question as to which prerequisites, circumstances and resources should be available so that the motivation and performance of employees can be maintained and, in the best case, even increased.

Both the technology acceptance model from ► Chap. 4 and the basic motives of motivation and the associated self determination theory will be applied later for the analysis of the qualitative and quantitative research in this thesis. The same applies to the jobs demands-resources model, which is quasi at the centre of the own surveys and analyses.

For our own survey in ► Chap. 8, qualitative interviews with various managers from different companies were evaluated. All interview partners have already had practical experience with the application of artificial intelligence technologies in their work and in their companies. From these explorative qualitative interviews,

1 the requirements for future activities and professions are derived that are and will be characteristic and relevant for working with and applying artificial intelligence. These requirements form the basis for the following quantitative survey of working people by means of a questionnaire. The questions and their meaning will be described in more detail at the appropriate point in the course of this study. The aim of the survey is to identify the required resources that employees expect from the company and from their managers in order to feel ready and equipped for the implementation and use of AI technologies.

In this context, the following analysis in ► Chap. 9 is therefore concerned with motivational aspects. According to the jobs demands-resources model, the "right" provision of resources can increase the motivation of employees to use AI technologies (in their jobs) and keep it at a positive and productive level. This analysis will subsequently be extended to the technology acceptance model. Likewise, the further analysis will identify which type of motivation (performance, connection, power) is fundamentally significant or even decisive in the use of AI in companies and professions. For this purpose, the basic motives of motivation presented in ► Chap. 5 and the self determination-theory will be used. Understanding this gives companies and responsible managers a clear orientation on how to best prepare and lead employees for the changes in the course of using AI technologies.

In order to make these findings applicable to practice, a guideline for AI implementation in companies will be formulated in the final part of this thesis, in ► Chap. 10. In accordance with the research question, this guideline refers to the recommended procedure for AI implementation in order to achieve the most productive and effective human-AI collaboration possible.

## Literature

Aggarwal, Charu C.: Machine Learning for Text, Cham 2018

Agrawal, A.; Gans, J.; Goldfarb, A.: Prediction machines. The simple economics of artificial intelligence, Harvard 2018

Bartneck, Christoph; Belpaeme, Tony; Eyssel, Friederike; Kanda, Takayuki; Keijsers, Merel; Šabanovi, Selma: Mensch-Roboter-Interaktion: Eine Einführung, München 2020

Brommer, D.; Hockling, S.; Leopold, A. (Hrsg.): Faszination New Work: 50 Impulse für die neue Arbeitswelt, Wiesbaden 2020

Butz, A.; Krüger, A.: Mensch-Maschine-Interaktion, Berlin/Boston 2017

Buxmann, Peter; Schmidt, Holger: Künstliche Intelligenz. Mit Algorithmen zum wirtschaftlichen Erfolg, Heidelberg 2019

Daugherty, P.; Wilson, J.H.: Human + Machine. Reimagining Work in the age of AI, Harvard 2018

Deloitte (Hrsg.): State of AI in the Enterprise, Düsseldorf 2020

Doherty, Conor; Camina, Steven; White, Kevin; Orenstein, Gary: The Path to Predictive Analytics and machine Learning, Boston 2016

Ertel, Wolfgang: Grundkurs Künstliche Intelligenz. Eine praxisorientierte Einführung, Wiesbaden 2018

Fraunhofer Institut (Hrsg.): Trends in Artificial Intelligence, München 2018

Geramanis, O.; Hermann, K. (Hrsg.): Führen in ungewissen Zeiten. Impulse, Konzepte und Praxisbeispiele, Wiesbaden 2016

Geramanis, O.; Hutmacher, S. (Hrsg.): Identität in der Modernen Arbeitswelt. Neue Konzepte für Zugehörigkeit, Zusammenarbeit und Führung, Wiesbaden 2018

Geramanis, O.; Hutmacher, S. (Hrsg): Der Mensch in der Selbstorganisation. Kooperationskonzepte für eine moderne Arbeitswelt, Wiesbaden 2020

Gerdenitsch, Cornelia; Korunka, Christian: Digitale Transformation der Arbeitswelt. Psychologische Erkenntnisse zur Gestaltung von aktuellen und zukünftigen Arbeitswelten, Heidelberg 2019

Goodfellow, Ian; Bengio, Yoshua; Courville, Aaron: Deep Learning, Frechen 2019

Hasenbein, Melanie: Der Mensch im Fokus der digitalen Arbeitswelt. Wirtschaftspsychologische Perspektiven und Anwendungsfelder, Heidelberg 2020

Igual, Laura; Segui, Santi: Introduction to data Science. A Python Approach to concepts, techniques and applications, Cham 2017

Independent High Level Expert Group on Artificial Intelligence: Ethics Guidelines for Trustworthy AI, Brüssel 2019

Kasparov, Garry: The Chess Master and the Computer, New York Review of Books, 2/2010

Lämmel, Uwe; Cleve, Jürgen: Künstliche Intelligenz. Wissensverarbeitung – Neuronale Netze, München 2020

Liggieri, K.; Müller, O.: Mensch-Maschine-Interaktion. Handbuch zu Geschichte, Kultur, Ethik, Berlin 2019

Manzeschke, Arne: MEESTAR. Ein Modell angewandter Ethik im Bereich assistiver Technologien, in: Weber, Karsten; Frommeld, Deborah; Manzeschke, Arne; Fangerau, Heiner (Hrsg.): Technisierung des Alltags. Beitrag für ein gutes Leben?, Stuttgart 2015

McKinsey Global Institute: Artificial Intelligence: The next digital frontier?, Brussels 2017

Münchner Kreis e.V., Bertelsmann Stiftung (Hrsg.) Leben, Arbeit, Bildung 2035+. Durch Künstliche Intelligenz beeinflusste Veränderungen in zentralen Lebensbereichen, München 2020

Oettinger, Michael: Data Science. Eine praxisorientierte Einführung im Umfeld von Machine Learning, Künstlicher Intelligenz und Big Data, Hamburg 2018

Plattform Lernende Systeme (Hrsg.): Von Daten zu Wertschöpfung. Potenziale von daten- und KI-basierten Wertschöpfungsnetzwerken, München 2020a

Plattform Lernende Systeme (Hrsg.): Kriterien für die Mensch-Maschine-Interaktion bei KI. Ansätze für die menschengerechte Gestaltung in der Arbeitswelt, München 2020b

Stanford University: Artfificial Intelligence Index Report 2019, Stanford 2020

University of Oxford et al.: The Malicious Use of Artificial Intelligence: Forecasting, Prevention and Mitigation, Oxford 2018

VanderPlas, Jake: Data Science mit Python, Frechen 2017

Wörwag, S.; Cloots, A. (Hrsg.): Human Digital Work – Eine Utopie? Erkenntnisse aus Forschung und Praxis zur digitalen Transformation der Arbeit, Wiesbaden 2020

# Man and Machine

## Contents




A. Moring, *AI on The Job*,
https://doi.org/10.1007/978-3-662-64005-0_2

2

Humans and machines have been interacting for many centuries. Machines have always been tools of man and controllable and under control by man. With the industrial revolution and digitalization, this relationship has become increasingly complex and dynamic, but has basically remained the same. With artificial intelligence, this will change. Machine and systems will become autonomous, self-learning and make decisions. Humans lose control and power when interacting with machines. In addition, there are a multitude of ethical questions to which we do not yet know the answers.

## 2.1 Human-Machine Interaction

The cooperation between humans and (intelligent) machines is the focus of this book. In particular, it will be examined how the technologies under the collective term of "artificial intelligence" (AI) affect the motivation of employees and their identification with their work. AI thus represents a new level of interaction between humans and machines, which will differ in many aspects from the previously known and experienced human-machine interaction. In order to understand and classify this, this short chapter will present the most important characteristics and the development of human-machine interaction from a scientific perspective.

Human-machine interaction (HMI) deals with the interaction between humans and machines. Synonymously or more related to communication, one also speaks of human-machine communication. In many cases the machine is a computer or contains information and communication technologies (ICT) and application or information systems. Therefore, there is a close relationship and considerable overlap with human-computer interaction (HCI). Recent products in which MMI has played a role include the touchscreen and data glasses.

### ▪ Human-Computer Interaction

As a narrower subfield of human-machine interaction, HCI deals with the user-friendly design of interactive systems and human-machine interfaces as well as with the usability of the software and hardware used. According to ISO 9241, the term user interface, which primarily refers to computer software and interactive media such as the Internet, comprises "all components of an interactive system that provide information and control elements necessary for the user to perform a specific task with the interactive system" (DIN EN ISO 9241, DIN e. V. Berlin).

The usability of user interfaces is then evaluated,

1. How accurately and completely users can achieve a particular goal – this is about effectiveness
2. What effort users have to make in relation to the accuracy and completeness of the effect achieved – this is about efficiency
3. How positive their attitude towards the use and how free it is of impairments – this is about satisfaction

Effectiveness, efficiency and satisfaction will also be the central criteria for measuring and evaluating the interaction between humans and AI-based systems in the context of this study. From a motivational point of view, these criteria are clearly interrelated. Satisfaction with one's own work situation promotes people's motivation and performance, as does the experience of being able to perform one's own work effectively and efficiently with the help of the technology or machine, i.e. being relieved by the machine in one's own work.

A more far-reaching question of human-machine interaction aims at the transferability of aspects of natural interaction between humans to machines (human-machine communication). The points of reference here are cognitive performances such as the understanding and production of language, gestures or facial expressions in dialogic interaction up to human-technology cooperation and its realization by artificial interlocutors as well as 'social' robots. We will already encounter these 'social robots' in the next chapter, when we will talk about AI-based 'intelligent agents'. Human-machine interaction is thus an interdisciplinary field for which, in addition to computer science and artificial intelligence research, insights from media psychology and design, from work science, software ergonomics, cognitive science and the sociology of technology are also relevant.

> The importance of human-machine interaction for practical application and implementation in companies will increase significantly in the coming years.

This is not only, but also due to the increasing use of artificial intelligence in companies. The deeper reason is the exponential growth of computing power of basically all machines around us humans. This is as true in the work environment as it is in our personal lives and private use. Likewise, the available storage space continues to grow exponentially. But: The biological conditions of humans remain essentially constant in comparison to this ever faster change. Biological evolution is, after all, much slower than technological evolution. This inevitably means that the functional and productive operation of machines and the cooperation between man and machine will become increasingly important. That is why the question of this book is also directed at how the conditions must be designed so that this cooperation can develop productively and efficiently at all, i.e. "function".

With the advent of the personal computer in the early 1980s, the number of users and applications of computer systems increased rapidly. Since then, the field of HCI has also developed with comparable dynamism and now includes a large number of different research directions, some of which go far beyond the classic industrial goal of optimizing the working environment for people. In this context, it is interesting to note that AI technologies in particular are intended to ensure more optimizations in existing processes and workflows in organizations, as will be explained in more detail later. This working definition is based on the original and continuing focus of HCI on the usability of the systems under consideration. On the one hand, the concept of usability is the unifying element between the now numerous directions and subfields of HCI; on the other hand, the concept itself has been continuously developed and redefined again and again by HCI. Thus, usability in the context of HCI no longer refers to the pure aspects of functionality and usability, but also includes aspects such as enjoyment, aesthetics, or creativity, among others (cf. Jacobsen and Meyer 2019). With the inclusion of these aspects, a bridge and connection can be made almost automatically to the models and

2

theories of motivation of people in their work environment. After all, enjoyment of work, an aesthetic sense of work in the sense of intuitive and comprehensible use of systems, and also the opportunity to be creative are proven motivators that will also emerge clearly in this study's own empirical survey. (See ▶ Chap. 8 "Expectations of Employees").

The origins of HCI lie in the field of computer science. The original focus was on the investigation and improvement of classical application fields, such as word processing or spreadsheets. In the course of its very dynamic development, HCI has been continuously extended by additional and new application fields. Among others, data visualization, information systems, collaborative systems, development environments for system development, and many areas of design have emerged as new focus areas of HCI. As a result of this expansion, HCI today has many points of connection and overlap with various fields and scientific disciplines. The concept of interaction always plays a central role in all of these areas.

#### ▪ Common Notion of Interaction

Despite the multi-layered aspects of HCI, however, a common concept of interaction can certainly be defined. The term interaction is used in many scientific disciplines. In physics, interaction refers to the interaction between elementary particles or, in general, the mutual interaction of systems. In biology, interaction is a functional term in an ecosystem and describes the effect of different organisms and substances on each other. In sociology and psychology, the interrelated action of two or more persons is referred to as interaction. Other uses of the term interaction can be found in fields as diverse as pharmacology, statistics, linguistics, political science, and even music. In the context of HCI, interaction is often defined as dialogue or communication between humans and computers. This definition of interaction is thus recognizably still strongly oriented towards the initial focus on classical productive applications. Although it is still sufficient and appropriate for the consideration of individual aspects of HCI, it no longer necessarily covers all aspects of HCI very well. For this reason, alternative definitions of the term interaction are proposed: interaction is the purposeful, reciprocal transfer of information between two or more entities.

At first glance, this definition does not seem too different from a definition of interaction as a dialogue between humans and computers. However, the new definition covers a wider range of circumstances and levels of abstraction. For example, the interaction of a user with a rotary switch can certainly be interpreted as a very simple transfer of information. To interpret such a process as a dialogue, on the other hand, does not seem accurate. A more abstract and thus more general definition, however, always runs the risk of becoming arbitrary. Not every information transfer is also an interaction. An example here would be the sending of human messages in various forms and media, which were sent into space in the 1970s with the Pioneer and Voyager space probes. This is a transfer of information, but not interaction in the sense of the above definition, because this transfer is neither reciprocal nor is there a goal beyond the mere transfer of information. Thus, an interaction in this sense does not only consist of the transfer of information between two or more entities, but also of a goal, which is to be aimed at with an information transfer in each case. In the abstract, such a goal can be understood as the sending entity wanting to change the current state of the receiving entity (Frey and Bierhoff 2011). The only means available to the sending entity for this is the transfer of information, which potentially changes the state of the receiving entity in the desired way. The property of reciprocity of interaction then makes it possible to actually check whether this goal has been achieved or not, or only partially.

### ■ Intuitive Operability of Systems and Devices

The concept of usability, especially in the early days of HCI, was described in a very simplistic way with the phrase "easy to learn, easy to use". Today, the core of this statement can be found in the concept of intuitive usability of systems and devices. This characteristic, which is the goal of virtually all interactive systems, is directly related to the structure of interactive systems. An interactive system consists of independent entities that purposefully and reciprocally influence their respective system states through the exchange of information. This schema describes one of the central challenges of interactive systems: The entities involved cannot directly observe the system states of the other entities. They can only indirectly estimate the respective states of the other entities with the help of the transferred information.

**Background Information**

Challenges of HCI

With respect to human-computer interaction, two central challenges for the development of interactive systems can be derived from this formal description:

- How can the system status of the computer system be estimated by the user?
- How can the "system state" of the user be estimated by the computer system?

These two defined challenges bring us to a crucial point when it comes to computer systems based on artificial intelligence in HCI. This is because the system state is very difficult, and in some cases even impossible, for the user to assess or comprehend due to the complexity and speed of the processes taking place and the enormous amounts of data. On the other hand, the second challenge is potentially quite easy to solve, because AI systems are very good and, with progressive development and use, increasingly better able to estimate, i.e. calculate, the "system states" of the respective users, if only sufficient data are available. At first glance, one could say that the machine or the computer has a clear advantage over the human user and partner when it comes to the two central challenges.

A large part of the complex aspects of HCI can be traced back to these two questions. An interactive system is intuitive and easy to use if the user can build up an internal model of the system and use this model to make correct predictions about the system's behavior. A system is more intuitive the faster the user can build this model. In the case of AI systems, it is therefore necessary to first provide users with a basic technical understanding of how various AI methods work before they are even able to build such a model for themselves. This is a thesis that arises from the above-mentioned considerations and that will be examined in the course of the study.

Designers of an interactive system can support this modeling process by exploiting natural and cultural models or expectations already present in the user through experience and habit. For example, a user from a Western culture processes visually presented, textual information from left to right and from top to bottom. In a corresponding context, the color green is intuitively associated with "All is well", the color red with "Caution" or "Warning". In another context, the color blue is associated with "cold" and the color red, in turn, with "warm". If the user sees a button, he will most likely assume that it can be pressed. If it is a slider, he is more likely to assume a different type of movement. Many of these models or expectations are processed unconsciously, and the user only notices if a system should act contrary to these expectations or react differently than usual.

In addition to these unconscious expectations, the consciously perceived structure and macroscopic behavior of the system should also be consistent and exhibit behavior that is predictable for humans. Here, too, the developers and designers of such an interactive system may be able to make use of the models already created in the users. For example, if the users already have experience with systems of a similar nature. In this case, the system should take up the already known structures and behavior patterns of these similar systems. An example of this are keyboard commands that are consistent across system boundaries for copying, cutting, and pasting to and from the clipboard (Ctrl-C, Ctrl-X, Ctrl-V) or for opening, saving, and printing files (Ctrl-O, Ctrl-S, Ctrl-P).

**Definition**

Intuitive systems

The definition of an intuitively operable system can be derived accordingly from these considerations: A system is intuitively operable if its behavior corresponds to the natural and cultural expectations already built into the user and supports the modeling of the system on the part of the user through consistent behavior that builds on the user's previous experience.

#### ▪ Ethical Issues of Artificial Intelligence

In addition to the described central aspects of human-machine or HCI, there are other aspects that play a special role in connection with AI systems and will presumably gain in importance and interest in the future. Artificial intelligence is currently associated with all kinds of utopian and dystopian expectations and forecasts. While one side sees a new stage of evolution in the collaboration of humans and artificial intelligence and praises the possibilities that are to arise from the combination of human, biological thinking and the intelligence of machines and systems (cf. Diamandis and Kotler 2020; Talwar 2020; Schneider 2019), the other side sees gloomy future scenarios looming. According to them, the threat of subjugation, if not extinction, by a new superintelligence, or at least further subjugation to the capitalist-industrial optimization logic of the online economy, potentiated by the power of autonomous systems (cf. Precht 2020). These antagonistic orientations of prognoses with regard to new machines and systems in the environment of humans are not new, but rather a typical concomitant of innovation and change thrusts at the latest since the industrial revolution and the mechanization of work (cf. Zill 2020).

Likewise, ethical issues and discussions run through the history of human-machine/computer interaction in theory and practice. With the emergence and proliferation of autonomous systems and AI-based applications, these ethical aspects have gained significant presence in recent years. In particular, safety issues are at the center of considerations and the question of what or to what extent machines or systems should be able to make their own "decisions" and where the unrestricted domain of humans in decisions and actions should be defined (Decker: Ethische Fragen bei autonomen Systemen; Lampe, Kaminski: Verlässlichkeit und Vertrauenswürdigkeit von Computersimulationen; Weydner-Volkmann: Sicherheitsfragen in der Mensch-Maschine-Interaktion, in: Liggieri, Müller: Mensch-Maschine-Interaktion (Decker: Ethical Issues in Autonomous Systems; Lampe, Kaminski: Reliability and Trustworthiness of Computer Simulations; Weydner-Volkmann: Security Issues in Human-Machine Interaction, in: Liggieri, Müller: Human-Machine Interaction.) 2020). Of course, these discussions are closely related to the utopian and dystopian future scenarios mentioned above, or are strongly influenced by them. These considerations do not only play a role on the scientific or (moral) philosophical level, but also very concretely in the strategies, considerations and expectations of companies and employees, as will become apparent in the qualitative and quantitative surveys and analyses of this study later in the book.

## Literature

Decker, Michael: Ethische Fragen bei autonomen Systemen; Hildrun Lampe, Andreas Kaminski: Verlässlichkeit und Vertrauenswürdigkeit von Computersimulationen; Sebastian Weydner-Volkmann: Sicherheitsfragen in der Mensch-Maschine-Interaktion, in: Kevin Liggieri, Oliver Müller: Mensch-Maschine-Interaktion. Handbuch zu Geschichte, Kultur, Ethik, Berlin 2020, S. 309–337

Diamandis, Peter; Kotler, Steven: The Future Is Faster Than You Think: How Converging Technologies Are Transforming Business, Industries, and Our Lives, New York 2020

Frey, Dieter; Bierhoff, Hans-Werner: Sozialpsychologie - Interaktion und Gruppe, Göttingen 2011

Jacobsen, Jens; Meyer, Lorena: Praxisbuch Usability und UX: Bewährte Usability- und UX-Methoden praxisnah erklärt, Bonn 2019

Precht, Richard David: KI und der Sinn des Lebens, Berlin 2020

Schneider, Susan: Artificial You: AI and the Future of Your Mind, Princeton 2019

Talwar, Rohit: Unleashing Human Potential: The Future of AI in Business, Los Angeles 2020

Zill, Rüdiger: Die Diktatur der Maschinen und die Antiquiertheit des Menschen; Kevin Liggieri: Anthropotechnik. Mensch und Maschine als (System-)Partner; Martina Heßler: Die Maschine als Konkurrentin im Mensch-Maschine-Vergleich, in: Kevin Liggieri, Oliver Müller: Mensch-Maschine-Interaktion. Handbuch zu Geschichte, Kultur, Ethik, Berlin 2020, S. 71–94, 134–164.

# Artificial Intelligence

Contents




A. Moring, *AI on The Job*,
https://doi.org/10.1007/978-3-662-64005-0_3

3

We can only understand the changes in workflows, processes and organizations brought about by AI if we know how artificial intelligence technologies and applications work. This helps us to get a realistic picture and to assess the possibilities correctly. As always with new technologies, hype and disappointment are close together. We overestimate the short-term effects and we underestimate the long-term effects. With AI, probably even a bit more so because the technology is quite complex and sophisticated. On top of that, there are several AI concepts, with their own strengths and weaknesses. Therefore, the most important functional and working methods are presented, explained and classified in the following.

## 3.1 What Is Artificial Intelligence?

This chapter provides an overview of the most important technologies and models that are commonly grouped under the term "artificial intelligence". The aim is to develop a basic understanding of how these technologies work and function, and to learn about use cases. It is also important to note that, despite the name, this is not a human-like form of intelligence in machines and systems, but primarily the optimization of various processes is the goal of AI applications. Technical contexts and details will also be discussed because they are necessary for understanding. On the basis of this knowledge, it will later be possible to clearly name and justify the challenges and changes that inevitably come to companies through the use of AI technologies and which also affect employees. On this basis, it will also be possible to carry out an analysis of employee motivation when it comes to the question of which factors and circumstances should be (particularly) taken into account when implementing AI technologies and what the correct procedure for this implementation should be. This analysis will then also make use of the models and theories presented later in this chapter.

**Definition**

Artificial intelligence

Artificial intelligence (AI) deals with methods that enable a computer to solve those tasks that, when solved by humans, require intelligence. The concept of artificial intelligence includes two basic aspects.

- On the one hand, it is understood as the creation and imitation of human behavior and thinking. This is the more ambitious and visionary goal.
- The second aspect is the automatic and autonomous task completion, which can take over clearly defined and delimited task areas.

The second aspect in particular will become relevant for companies in the short term, or already is, and will change working life, processes and tasks in companies. We know examples of autonomous task completion: Autonomous driving, intelligent software assistants in companies or also for private use in apps or directly on the smartphone, as well as automatic voice and image recognition. These systems already work very reliably and are increasingly integrating into our everyday lives. Feature of both approaches of AI is the independent learning and processing of new and unknown data. New information flows into the internal model, which then leads to the adaptation of the system to new environmental conditions and requirements.

The ever-increasing convergence of Big Data with AI is currently the most important development influencing how companies will achieve business value from their data and their analytical capabilities in the future. Artificial intelligence and machine learning are currently used interchangeably. Both terms pop up regularly when talking about Big Data, analytics and the broader impact of technological change. With both, the real value to the business is in the data, without which any AI would have "no fodder," so to speak, for learning and ongoing optimization, adaptation, and control.

**Background Information**

Recognize patterns, make decisions

Artificial intelligence is thus the umbrella term for applications in which machines perform human-like intelligence tasks such as learning, judgment, and problem solving. Machine learning (ML) technology – a subfield of artificial intelligence – teaches computers to learn from data and experience and to perform tasks ever better. Sophisticated algorithms can recognize patterns in unstructured data sets such as images, text, or spoken language and make decisions on their own based on these patterns (Cf. Doherty et al. 2016; Ertel 2018; Kaplan 2017; Agarwal 2018).

Machine learning occurs either through training using a data set with already known outputs ("supervised learning"), or algorithms must themselves recognize patterns in data ("unsupervised learning"). Learning by reward and punishment ("reinforced or reinforcement learning") is also possible, where the algorithm independently detects whether the learning component benefits the entire system (reward) or not (punishment). The data is either structured, for example in table form, or unstructured as text, images or speech – as in the case of emails or social media posts. Machine learning can in principle process all data, which is of course a great advantage.

### ▪ And Where Does That Leave Us Humans?

We humans tend to think a system is intelligent whenever and as long as we don't know exactly how it works. At the same time, this is exactly what is scary for us and makes us feel insecure. When there was no computer that could beat professional chess players, people were convinced that a system had to be really "intelligent" if it could actually beat the best people in chess by itself. After the system was built (IBM's DeepBlue) and could beat the best chess players in the world, perceptions quickly turned around that it was after all just a sophisticated algorithm combined with a lot of computing power. So our attitude to AI and our assessment of its impact on us and our lives and work can change as a result of experience and familiarisation.

Similarly, there are many other problems that today can seemingly be solved as a matter of course with AI algorithms, but for which not so long ago we were certain that intelligence was required to solve them. So, on the one hand, the perception of intelligence depends on whether we have a complete understanding of the way the solution is found. On the other hand, intelligence always relates to a particular problem, and people are very good at using their intelligence to solve very many different kinds of problems. Above all, it is important to have an understanding of how artificial intelligence technologies and processes work and what rules and principles they follow. Only those who know the rules can play and judge a game. Understanding and knowledge is the indispensable basis for sovereignty, security and decision-making ability. It is also the basis for shaping change and innovation and for leading companies in times of dynamic change.

## 3.2 Machine Learning

An important feature of artificial intelligence systems is their ability to learn on their own. Classic software works like this: Problems and questions are processed based on predetermined rules. In contrast, self-learning machine learning algorithms can learn the best rules for solving certain tasks themselves. Here, so-called neural networks play a central role, which will be described in more detail later. An artificial neural network consists of many individual neurons, which are usually arranged in several interconnected layers. The number of layers determines, among other things, the degree of complexity that an artificial neural network can represent. Many layers make a neural network "deep" – this is why we also talk about deep learning as a subcategory of machine learning in this context.

> Important in the so-called supervised machine learning is the fact that in this method the correct result is known to us humans because we know the input data that is fed into the machine or the neural network.

Input data can be, for example, numbers or objects or words. However, the network or the machine does not "know" the correct result, is blank, so to speak, and is now supposed to "learn" it. Learning then works in the following way (cf. Rashid 2016; Raschka and Mirjalili 2018): After the network structure has been built, each neuron is given a random initial weight. Then, the input data is given to the network, and each neuron weights the input signals with its weight and passes the result to the neurons of the next layer (layer). Finally, at the last and final output layer of the network, the overall result is calculated. This will usually have little to do with the known actual result, since all neurons have a random initial weight. However, one can calculate the size of the error, and the proportion that each neuron had in that error, and then change the weight of each neuron a tiny bit in the direction that minimizes the error. Then the next pass occurs, another measurement of the error and adjustment of the weights, and so on. This is how a neural network slowly but surely "learns" to infer the known output data from the input data.

On one side of the neural network, the input data is fed in. Each input signal is distributed to each neuron of the first layer. Each neuron then weights the incoming signal with an input-specific weight, which was randomly assigned at the beginning, adds a so-called neuron-specific bias term and sums all input data weighted to the extent to the output of this neuron. Often, the output is still guided by a non-linear activation function in this process, for example to enforce a certain range of values of the output (cf. Rashid 2016; Raschka and Mirjalili 2018). Usually, sigmoid or Tanh functions are used for this purpose. The output of each neuron is then passed as input to all neurons in the following layer. This process continues until the output layer is reached, which provides the result of all computations.

So no learning process has taken place yet. Since all weights are randomly chosen within a given range of values (e.g. between −1 and 1) when a neural network is initialized, the result will be a completely random value. This is where the familiar "correct" results or examples mentioned in the beginning come into play. An example in this case means a combination of real input-output data pairs. These examples are used in the training of artificial neural networks to optimally set all weights and bias terms, so that at the end of the training the network can calculate the correct result for all input data and also for new input data not seen before. For a set of input data (also called features), the still untrained neural network calculates one result at a time. This result is then compared with the known results of the example data set (also called targets or labels), and then the size of the deviation or error is calculated.

#### ▪ The Actual "Learning" of the Machine

Now the actual "learning" begins: the measured error is fed backwards into the artificial neural network (the so-called backward pass or backward propagation), and each weight and bias term is adjusted a small bit in the direction that makes the error smaller (cf. Rashid 2016; Raschka and Mirjalili 2018). The magnitude of this adjustment is calculated first by the proportion that a given neuron weight had in the result (i.e., by its current weight), and second by the so-called learning rate, which is one of the most important adjustment variables (hyperparameters) of neural networks. Common learning rates are e.g. 0.001 or 0.01. This means: Only one hundredth to one thousandth of the calculated error is corrected per run. If the adjustment per run is too large, the minimum of the error curve may be missed and the deviations become larger instead of smaller. This is called "overshooting". Sometimes the learning rate is therefore increasingly reduced during training in order to better determine the minimum of the error function.

After all weights have been adjusted, a new run of all input data takes place and the error is measured again as well as the back propagation of this error for the renewed adjustment of the weights. A complete run of all input data is called an epoch. Here, depending on the size of the dataset, the input data can also be divided into groups of equal size (batches), and the training can be performed per batch at a time (cf. Kaplan 2017; Aggarwal 2018). This can be useful, for example, to allow an artificial neural network to learn faster, or to adhere to limitations on the computational capacity of the executing computer. The more examples an artificial neural network is given for training, and the more times it has seen them, the smaller the error in the results. There is one danger: If a neural network has seen all known data very often during training, the artificial neural network may learn this data by heart rather than learning an abstract concept. This problem is also known as overfitting. Since neural networks can also map highly complex functions, there is a risk that they will eventually have found the perfect function for every known data point, but that this function will not work well for new data (cf. Ertel 2018).



#### ▪ Checking the "Learning Success" with Test Data

To ensure that a network can abstract from known sample data and also provide correct results for previously unlearned input data, the sample data is divided into training data, test data, and blind test data before training, e.g., in the ratio 70/20/10. During training, only the training data is then used, and the error rate is measured for both the training data and the test data, respectively. However, the measured error of the test data is not fed back into the network. Then, the neural network is improved by adjusting all variables so that it achieves the maximum performance with respect to both training and test data. Only when the network is supposedly fully trained does the blind test data come into play. If the artificial neural network also performs well in the blind test, there is a high probability that it has learned an abstract concept well.

When the artificial neural network is finished training, all weights and biases are stored as a so-called "checkpoint"(cf. Kreutzer and Sirrenberg 2019). The neural network can then be restarted with these at any time. The actual operation of a trained neural network is much simpler and faster than the learning process beforehand and can therefore also be performed in near real-time on mobile devices or normal computers, for example. A fully trained artificial neural network can be retrained with new data at any time, since the "checkpoints" are already known. It is also possible to use a pre-trained neural network as a basis for training with your own data. In this so-called fine-tuning of artificial neural networks, general structures that have already been learned can be used and the network only has to learn the new classes. This is particularly useful in the very computationally intensive processing of large data sets, both images and speech and text or other types of data. Pre-trained artificial neural networks or customizable API services are now offered by IBM, Microsoft, Amazon, Google, Uber, Facebook and other service providers.

> For the described supervised learning, a large amount of example data is required as described. A large amount here means, for example, a million examples. Although artificial neural networks can sometimes achieve useful results with smaller data sets, the more data available, the better.

Supervised learning itself can be further subdivided into different methods of data use and data transfer within artificial neural networks. In so-called recurrent neural networks, for example, the result of the previous input data flows into the calculation of the current output. For example, time series and texts can be analyzed and processed. The same is true for long-short-term-memory networks (LSTM) and

Sequence-to-Sequence networks, which are used for speech recognition and for the translation of texts, among other things (cf. Kramer 2016; Ertel 2018). For image processing, so-called convolutional neural networks (CNN) are used, which scan images with a grid and abstract further from lower levels (points, lines, etc.) in each layer to higher concepts (a face, a house, etc.).

Other methods of how artificial neural networks can learn are unsupervised learning, in which systems only receive input data and attempt to classify it meaningfully themselves. In this context, we talk about "strong AI". Unsupervised machine learning algorithms infer patterns from a data set without reference to known or labelled outcomes. Unlike supervised machine learning, unsupervised machine learning cannot be applied directly to a regression or classification problem because you have no idea what the values for the output data might be, making it impossible for you to train the algorithm as you normally would. Unsupervised learning can be used instead to discover the underlying structure of the data (see Russel and Norvig 2016).

Unsupervised machine learning purports to uncover previously unknown patterns in data, but most of the time these patterns are poor approximations of what supervised machine learning can achieve. Also, since you don't know what the results should look like, there's no way to determine how accurate they are, making supervised machine learning more applicable to real-world problems. The best time to use unsupervised machine learning is when there is no data on the desired outcomes, such as determining a target market for a brand new product that a company has never sold before.

**Background Information**

Unsupervised machine learning some applications of unsupervised machine learning techniques are:

- Clustering allows you to automatically divide the dataset into groups based on similarity. However, cluster analysis often overestimates the similarity between groups and does not treat data points as individuals (see Rashid 2016; Kaplan 2017; Wartala 2018; Yao et al. 2019). For this reason, cluster analysis tends to be a poor choice for applications such as customer segmentation and targeting.
- Anomaly detection can automatically detect unusual data points in your dataset (see Rashid 2016; Kaplan 2017; Wartala 2018; Yao et al. 2019). This is useful for detecting fraudulent transactions, detecting faulty hardware, or identifying an outlier caused by a human error in data entry.
- Association mining identifies groups of items that frequently occur together in your dataset (see Rashid 2016; Kaplan 2017; Wartala 2018; Yao et al. 2019). Retailers often use it for shopping cart analysis, as it allows analysts to discover goods that are frequently purchased at the same time and develop more effective marketing and merchandising strategies.
- Latent variable models are often used for data preprocessing, e.g. to reduce the number of features in a data set (dimensionality reduction) or to decompose the data set into several components.

The patterns that can be uncovered using unsupervised machine learning methods can also prove useful in the subsequent implementation of supervised machine learning methods. For example, you can use an unsupervised technique to perform cluster analysis on the data, and then use the cluster to which each row belongs as an additional feature in the supervised machine learning model (semi-supervised machine learning). Another example is a fraud detection model that uses anomaly detection scores as an additional feature.

**Definition**

Reinforcement learning

Reinforcement learning also belongs to unsupervised or autonomous learning. In reinforcement learning, a neural network itself can control the input data (e.g., the buttons of a gaming controller) and receive dynamic output data back together with a task regarding this output data (e.g., maximize a score) (cf. Lapan 2020).



In contrast to the other two methods (supervised and unsupervised learning), reinforcement learning does not require any data in advance. Instead, they are generated and labeled in a simulation environment in many runs in a trial-and-error process during training.

Reinforcement learning stands for a whole series of individual methods in which a software agent independently learns a strategy. The goal of the learning process is to maximize the number of rewards within a simulation environment. During training, the agent performs actions within this environment at each time step and receives feedback on each action. In this process, the software agent is not shown in advance which action is best in which situation. Rather, it receives a reward at certain points in time. During training, the agent learns to assess the consequences of actions on situations in the simulation environment. On this basis, he can develop a long-term strategy to maximize the reward.

A so-called "policy"is then the learned behavior of a software agent. A policy specifies which action should be executed for any given behavioral variant (observation) from the learning environment (environment) in order to maximize the reward (cf. Ertel 2018; Lapan 2020). How can such a policy be mapped? For example, a so-called Q-table can be used for this purpose. In it, a table is built with all possible observations as rows and all possible actions as columns. The cells are then filled with the so-called value values during training, which represent the expected future reward. However, using the Q-table also has its limitations: it only works if the action and observation space remains small (cf. Graesser and Keng 2019; Lapan 2020). That is, when the action options and behavioral possibilities are small. If many features or even features with continuous values are to be evaluated by the software agent of, a neural network is needed to map the values. A common method for this is Deep Q-Learning. In detail, so-called neural networks are defined here with the features of the observation space as input layer and with the actions as output layer or output layer (cf. Wartala 2018). The values are then learned and stored in the individual neurons of the network during training.

### ▪ Neural Networks

**Definition**

Neural networks

The basis and, so to speak, the most important basic technology for Machine Learning and Artificial Intelligence are neural networks. A neural network is a collection of individual information processing units called neurons.

They are arranged in layers in a so-called network architecture. The neurons – also called nodes – of an artificial neural network are arranged layer by layer in so-called layers and are usually connected in a fixed hierarchy (cf. Rashid 2016; Goodfellow et al. 2019; Lämmel and Cleve 2020). Neurons are mostly connected between two layers, but in rarer cases also within a layer. Between layers or strata, each neuron of one layer is always connected to all neurons of the next layer. Starting with the input layer at the beginning, information flows through one or more hidden layers to the output layer at the end. The output of one neuron is the input of the next.

The number of layers of a neural network is an important descriptive information. For example, if a network contains 3 layers, it is called a 3-layer network. The input layer is the starting point of the information flow in an artificial neural network. Input signals are received by the neurons at the beginning of this layer and weighted at the end and passed on to the neurons of the first intermediate layer. In this process, a neuron of the input layer passes the respective information to all neurons of the first intermediate layer. Between the input and the output layer there is at least one hidden layer in each artificial neural network. Theoretically, the number of possible hidden layers in an artificial neural network is unlimited. In practice, however, each additional hidden layer also causes an increase in the computing power required to run the network. The output layer lies behind the intermediate layers and forms the final layer in an artificial neural network. Neurons located in the output layer are each connected to all neurons in the last intermediate layer. The output layer represents the end point of the information flow in an artificial neural network and contains the result of the information processing by the network.

#### ■ "Weights" Bring the Network Autonomously to the Optimal Solution

The so-called "weights"describe the intensity of the information flow along a connection in a neural network. For this purpose, each neuron assigns a weight to the information flowing through it and then passes this on to the neurons of the next layer, weighted and after the addition of a value for the neuron-specific bias. Typically, the weights and biases are initialized at the beginning of training in the range of values between $-1$ and 1, but can later be well outside this range. The result of the weights and biases is often passed through a so-called activation function (e.g.: sigmoid or tanh) before it is passed on to the neurons of the next layer.

The weights and biases are adjusted during the training process so that the final result matches the requirements as closely as possible. The simplest form of a neural network is the so-called "perceptron". In its original basic form, this type of network contains only a single neuron (perceptron) with adjustable weights and a threshold. There are a variety of other formulas of neural networks beyond this simplest form (cf. Goodfellow et al. 2019; Lämmel and Cleve 2020). Feedforward networks follow feedforward logic: information is passed in one direction ("forward") from the input layer through intermediate layers to the output layer. In addition, there are variants in which additional connections exist through which information can also traverse certain areas of the network backwards or again.

These networks are called recurrent networks, feedback networks or feedback networks.

Different variants are possible (cf. Rashid 2016; Goodfellow et al. 2019):

- direct feedback (a neuron uses its output as a new input)
- indirect feedback (the output of a neuron is used as input of a neuron in an upstream layer)
- lateral feedback (the output of a neuron is used as input of a neuron in the same layer)
- complete connection (the output of a neuron is used as additional input by every other neuron in the network)

**Background Information**

Recurrent networks

Recurrent networks are particularly necessary when sequential information processing is involved (sequence-to-sequence networks). This is the case, for example, in handwriting recognition, speech recognition and machine translation. Networks used to perform these tasks are usually based on direct feedback.

The Convolutional Neural Network (CNN) is widely used, especially in the field of image and audio processing (cf. Rashid 2016; Goodfellow et al. 2019). Typically, such a Convolutional Neural Network consists of at least 5 layers. Within each of these layers, pattern recognition is performed. Each layer thereby refines the pattern recognition based on the output of the previous layer. This process can be thought of as a small recognition grid that moves piece by piece over the area of the data set to be analyzed. In the case of an image, for example, this is done at the pixel level by analyzing small sections of the image (e.g., 2 × 2 pixels).

A Convolutional Neural Network is a Deep Learning architecture specifically designed for processing images. However, Convolutional Neural Networks are also extremely well suited for many other areas, such as text processing. A Convolutional Neural Network uses its filters to recognize structures in the respective input data in a location-independent manner (cf. Yao et al. 2019; Lämmel and Cleve 2020). On the first level, the filters are activated by simple structures such as lines, edges, and color spots. The type of filters is not predefined, but learned by the network. In the next level, structures are learned that consist of the combination of these basic structures, for example curves, simple shapes and so on. Thus, with each filter level, the abstraction level of the network increases. Which abstractions eventually lead to the activation of the posterior layers is determined by the characteristic features of the given classes to be recognized. Exactly how a Convolutional Network achieves these amazing results is not yet fully explained in mathematical theory (cf. Rashid 2016; Wartala 2018; Yao et al. 2019). However, it is clear that Convolutional Neural Networks currently achieve the best results in the field of image processing.

**Background Information**

Autonomous image and text recognition.

When it comes to recognizing objects in images, the performance of Convolutional Neutral Networks is already better than that of humans. Google's Deepmind also used CNN's for the famous AlphaGo system to evaluate the current game position of the Go board. This leads to another strength of these networks, which is their ability to condense information that exists as a matrix into a meaningful vector (see Rashid 2016; Wartala 2018; Yao et al. 2019). This property can be equally well exploited in the field of text processing. Current applications of Convolutional Neural Networks range from auto-encoders to object recognition in images and videos to synthetic generation of images and text from vectors. Research is currently being conducted in many other areas to determine whether CNNs can also achieve better results there than normal neural networks. There are hardly any limits to creativity due to the possibility of using matrix inputs.

A Convolutional Neural Network processes the input in the form of a matrix. Thus, it is possible to use images represented as a matrix (the matrix dimensions are width x height x color channels) as input. A normal neural network, for example in the form of a multi-layer perceptron (MLP), on the other hand, requires a vector as input. Thus, to use an image as input, the pixels of the image would have to be arranged in a long chain one after the other, which is called "flattening" in technical language (cf. Rashid 2016; Wartala 2018; Yao et al. 2019). As a result, normal neural networks are unable to recognize objects in an image regardless of the object's position in the image. The same object at a different position in the image would have a completely different input vector.

#### ■ Filter in Folded Net

A CNN essentially consists of filters (called convolutional layer) and aggregation layers (called pooling layer) that repeat alternately, and at the end one or more layers of "normal" fully connected neurons (called dense or also fully connected layer). The matrix input is first analyzed by a fixed number of so-called filters, which have a fixed pixel size (e.g., 2 × 2 or 3 × 3), and which then scan over the input's pixel matrix like a window with a constant step size. The filters move from left to right across the input matrix and jump to the next lower row after each pass. The so-called padding is used to determine how the filter should behave when it reaches the edge of the matrix.

The filter has a fixed weight for each point in its viewport, and it calculates a result matrix from the pixel values in the current viewport and these weights. The size of this result matrix depends on the size of the filter, the padding and especially the step size. For example, a step size of 2 for a filter size of 2 × 2 leads to a halving of the size of the result matrix per filter compared to the input matrix. In this case, each pixel is necessarily no longer connected to the filter individually, but 4 pixels are connected to the filter simultaneously (local connectivity). The input was thus "folded", hence the name convolutional network.

In the first layer of a CNN, a convolutional layer with 32 or 16 filters is usually used, whose convolutional output is a new matrix (cf. Goodfellow et al. 2019; Lämmel and Cleve 2020). This first layer is usually followed by a second convolutional layer of the same structure, which takes as input the new matrices from the convolution of the first layer. This is followed by a pooling layer. A pooling layer aggregates the results of convolutional layers by passing on only the strongest signal. For example, a MaxPooling Layer always uses the highest value of a kernel matrix and discards all others. The four matrix results produced by a 2 × 2 kernel are thus reduced to only one number (the highest of the four). Pooling is used to pass only the most relevant signals to the next layers, to achieve a more abstract representation of the content and to reduce the number of parameters of a network.

Many CNNs consist of a sequence of two convolutional layers each with the same number of filters, followed by a pooling layer, which in turn is followed by two convolutional layers and a pooling layer. While the size of the input is reduced by the convolutional layers and the pooling, the number of filters for the detection of higher-level signals is increased. The last pooling layer is therefore followed by one or more fully connected layers. The Fully Connected Layer or Dense Layer is a normal neural network structure in which all neurons are connected to all inputs and all outputs (cf. Yao et al. 2019; Lämmel and Cleve 2020). In order to feed the matrix output of the convolutional and pooling layers into a dense layer, the latter must first be rolled out (flattening). The output signals of the filter layers are independent of the position of an object, therefore position features are no longer available, but location-independent object information is. This object information is therefore fed into one or more Fully Connected Layers and connected to an output layer, which has, for example, exactly the number of neurons that corresponds to the number of different classes to be recognized.

In CNN, the results of each layer are in most cases activated by a so-called ReLU function (cf. Yao et al. 2019; Lämmel and Cleve 2020). This ReLU function ensures that all values smaller than zero become zero and all values larger than zero are preserved 1:1. The last layer receives a softmax activation in the case of classification problems, that is, the output of all output neurons adds up to 1 and gives the probability of the corresponding output in each case. The weights of the filters and the fully connected layers are randomly chosen at the beginning and then continuously optimized during training by backpropagation. In the case of classification problems (when it has to be clarified which object is visible in the image), the categorical cross-entropy is used in this process to measure the error (cf. Yao et al. 2019; Lämmel and Cleve 2020). This is the negative natural logarithm of the calculated probability for the category.

### ▪ Intelligent Agents

**Definition**

Intelligent agents

Intelligent agents are already very good at solving certain problems. In fact, they can often do it much faster and better than humans. Intelligent agents are not self-learning systems, because an intelligent agent is based on fixed algorithms, but it independently finds the solution to any problem in its domain, even if it has never seen it before. The strategies used for such intelligent agents are the basis for many applications and advancements of artificial intelligence and self-learning systems (see Doherty et al. 2016; Russel and Norvig 2016; Kreutzer and Sirrenberg 2019).

The basic strategy of artificial agents can be well illustrated by the example of various games or puzzles. Let us start with the number puzzle Sudoku. In a table with 9 × 9 fields, which is divided into 9 sub-tables with 3 × 3 fields each, the numbers from 1–9 are to be entered in such a way that in each row and each column and in each sub-table each number occurs only once. This restriction provides a relatively clear solution path for simple Sudokus, as long as one always has all columns, rows and sub-tables and the numbers already used in each case in view. From the already existing numbers per row, column and sub-table results a restriction of the possibility-space (constraint) for the remaining empty fields of the respective category. This means that only certain numbers remain that can be used for these fields.
The first strategy of an intelligent Sudoku agent is therefore to have an always up-to-date overview of the numbers still possible per empty field. Whenever a new number can be entered, the possibility space of the remaining empty fields is updated accordingly, as far as they are affected. This strategy is called constraint propagation (see Doherty et al. 2016; Russel and Norvig 2016; Ertel 2018; Wartala 2018; Lämmel and Cleve 2020). Simple Sudokus, where there is always at least one unique next empty square, can be solved using this strategy alone. However, in more difficult Sudokus, one often reaches points where there is no clear next step, but two or more possibilities, but only one of them is correct. Humans and machines use a second strategy at this point: Search.

If an intelligent agent is presented with more than one option for the next step, it starts trying out all the options one after the other (Kreutzer and Sirrenberg 2019). The selection of the search algorithm and an evaluation function for the available options determines the search order and thus also the efficiency and speed of the search. One of the simplest variants in this context is depth-first search (cf. Doherty et al. 2016; Russel and Norvig 2016; Ertel 2018; Wartala 2018; Lämmel and Cleve 2020). This is a search algorithm that always searches the available decision trees first towards possible end goals. That is, each branch is first searched to the end before the next branch takes its turn. In contrast, the breadth-first search variant searches each level of the decision tree completely before searching one level lower. Both variants are so-called brute force strategies. In these strategies, one tries to solve a problem with sheer computational power by simply calculating all possible variants to the end. If the search space is simply too large for this, more complex and powerful search algorithms such as uniform cost search and A-Star search are used (cf. Doherty et al. 2016; Russel and Norvig 2016; Ertel 2018; Wartala 2018; Lämmel and Cleve 2020). Furthermore, constraint propagation can also be improved by further restricting the possibility spaces using, for example, the Naked Twins strategy: If two fields in the aforementioned Sudoku example each have only the same two numbers as their current possibility space, it is not known to which field which number belongs, but it is clear that all other fields within the affected rows, columns and sub-tables cannot contain this number. Both numbers can therefore be deleted accordingly from the possibility spaces of all other affected fields.

**Background Information**

How an intelligent agent works.

So then, the intelligent agent's Sudoku algorithm works as follows in one run:

1. Constraint propagation: Update of the possibility spaces
2. OnlyChoice: Fill fields where there is a unique choice
3. NakedTwins: Apply further restriction to the possibility spaces.
4. Search: Select the field with the fewest possibilities, reapply the above strategies including search until a solution or error is returned.



Searching and narrowing the possibility space are efficient strategies that specialized intelligent agents can use to solve diverse problems intelligently. Even if they are "only" algorithms, these agents are undeniably very intelligent in solving the problems of their specialized domain and, above all, much faster, more reliable and better than human agents. A special detail in the matter: for certain tasks, the development of intelligent agents can also lead to the fact that people who previously found this task interesting and enjoyed solving it, have little interest in solving it manually afterwards. The good old pocket calculator is a perfect example of how something like this looks quite practically in all of our daily lives. New technologies, especially if they are or even appear complicated, are first marveled at or resented and then, under certain conditions and prerequisites, accepted and adapted until they finally form an integral part of our consumption and work behavior. It is precisely these conditions and prerequisites for this that are the subject of the following chapter.

## Literature


Agarwal, P. K.: Public Administration Challenges in the World of AI and Bots. Public Administration Review. Nov/Dec 2018, Vol. 78 Issue 6, p917–921. 5p. 1 Black and White Photograph.

Aggarwal, Charu C.: Machine Learning for Text, Cham 2018

Doherty, Conor; Camina, Steven; White, Kevin; Orenstein, Gary: The Path to Predictive Analytics and machine Learning, Boston 2016

Ertel, Wolfgang: Grundkurs Künstliche Intelligenz. Eine praxisorientierte Einführung, Wiesbaden 2018

Goodfellow, Ian; Bengio, Yoshua; Courville, Aaron: Deep Learning, Frechen 2019

Graesser, Laura; Keng, Wah Loon: Foundations of Deep Reinforcement Learning: Theory and Practice in Python, Boston 2019

Kaplan, Jerry: Künstliche Intelligenz. Eine Einführung, Frechen 2017

Kramer, O.: Machine learning for evolution strategies. Studies in big data. Cham 2016

Kreutzer, Ralf; Sirrenberg, Marie: Künstliche Intelligenz verstehen. Grundlagen – Use-Cases – unternehmenseigene KI-Journey, Wiesbaden 2019

Lämmel, Uwe; Cleve, Jürgen: Künstliche Intelligenz. Wissensverarbeitung – Neuronale Netze, München 2020

Lapan, Maximilian: Deep Reinforcement Learning, Frechen 2020

Raschka, Sebastian; Mirjalili, Vahid: Machine Learning mit Python und Scikit-learn und TensorFlow, Frechen 2018

Rashid, Tariq: Neuronale Netze selbst programmieren, Heidelberg 2016

Russel, Stuart; Norvig, Peter: Artificial Intelligence: A Modern Approach, Essex 2016

Wartala, Ramon: Praxiseinstieg Deep Learning, Heidelberg 2018

Yao, Haipeng; Jiang, Chunxiao; Qian, Yi: Developing Networks using Artificial Intelligence, Cham 2019.

# Theories of Technical Adaptation

Contents




A. Moring, *AI on The Job*,
https://doi.org/10.1007/978-3-662-64005-0_4

4

There is a multitude of theories on the question of how and why technologies are used and develop their effects. In their basic features, they are largely similar or even congruent. The difference usually lies in the focus and weighting of individual factors and details. This chapter provides an overview of different models that deal with the adaptation and acceptance of technical innovations or new technologies. These theories examine the conditions and circumstances that motivate people to engage with new technological applications and technologies, to learn and apply them, and to work productively and efficiently. The question of motivation thus plays a central role here.

While the psychological models direct their attention and focus on the inner constitution of a person in dependence of the social circumstances and in connection with an existing or denied need satisfaction, the focus of the theories and models presented here is on the human-machine or human-technology interaction.

For this coherent reason, these theories will be presented first, before the following chapter deals with the more human-individual focused motivation theories of (work and personnel) psychology. The focus of the presentation will be on the so-called Technology Acceptance Model, as it is closest to the question posed in this book.

- **The Importance of Acceptance**

Generally, acceptance is defined as "an antagonism to the notion of denial and means the positive decision to adopt an innovation" (Simon 2001) Decision makers in organizations should know the aspects of acceptance that influence users' decision to adopt a particular system so that they can consider them in the development and implementation phases. Thus, the question for both practitioners and researchers is why people accept new technologies. Answering this question can help in finding better methods to design, evaluate and predict user response to the new technologies. Models and theories of technology acceptance have been applied in a variety of areas to understand and predict people's behavior in such diverse contexts as voting, dieting, family planning, blood donation, women's career orientation, breast cancer screening, transportation choices, sales projections, birth control pill use, sexual education, consumer purchasing behavior, and computer use. In the field of technology acceptance, different theories and frameworks have been developed to evaluate the use of certain developed and implemented technologies. Basically, more than one theoretical approach is also necessary for a complete understanding of the issues involved. The individual approaches with their focus in turn provide more clarity with respect to individual aspects of technology acceptance.

## 4.1 Theory of Reasoned Action

Although the TRA model was first developed and applied to sociological and psychological questions by Fishbein and Aiizen in 1975, in recent years it has been primarily used to study the IT usage behavior of individuals (cf. Moore and

Benbasat 1991; Kuo et al. 2015). In this model, human behavior is predicted and explained by three main cognitive components. These are a person's attitudes (a person's feeling of disadvantage or favour for the behaviour), social norms (social influence of the general environment) and intentions (an individual's decision to behave in a certain way or not). According to the theory, this human behavior should always be volitional, rational and systematic. Furthermore, there are three limiting factors to test and evaluate TRA: volitional control, stability of intention over time, and measurement of intention in terms of goal, time, context, action, and specificity. In addition, criteria such as generality, goal, action, context, and time horizon are established to describe the robustness between corresponding intention and attitude. Weaknesses of the Theory of Reasoned Action are the lack of addressing the importance of habits, cognitive deliberation, misunderstanding in questioning (attitudes, subjective norms and intentions of respondents) and moral factors.

## 4.2 Theory of Planned Behaviour

In this model, perceived behavioral control (PBC) is added as a new variable to extend the TRA model. This PBC is fundamentally determined by the availability of resources, opportunities, and abilities as well as the perceived importance of these resources, opportunities, and abilities in achieving outcomes (cf. Ajzen 1991; Mathieson 1991). Although both TPB and TRA assume that behavioral intentions influence an individual's behavior, the Theory of Planned Behavior and the concept of behavioral control (PBC) assume that individuals' actions are not under the arbitrary control of the individual. By adding behavioral control, TRA sets realistic limits, so to speak. Moreover, this behavioral control has both a direct influence on actual behavior and an indirect influence by affecting behavioral intentions. Therefore, in the TPB model, three main factors influence personal behavior: the described behavioral control, subjective norms, and behavioral attitude of the person. However, there are two criticisms of the TPB model (see Taherdoost et al. 2011a, b) in relation to technology acceptance. First, the individual's own attitude towards information technology is considered largely irrelevant. Secondly, the model does not sufficiently consider whether and how adapted framework conditions influence the degree of voluntariness with which people engage with technologies.

## 4.3 Theory of Interpersonal Behaviour

This model attempts to describe the complexity of human behavior using social and emotional factors. Therefore, this model not only includes all aspects of TRA and TPB, but also facilitates predicting conditions and effects by including habits of people. The concept of social factors includes role models, norms, and self-concepts, which is similar to the subjective norm construct in TRA (see Fishbein and Ajzen 2001). According to the Theory of interpersonal Behaviour, the individual is neither fully deliberative nor fully automatic, further neither fully autonomous nor fully social. TRA and TIB thus differ in the sense that TRA is interested in describing the greatest variance with the fewest variables, whereas TIB is interested in accounting for the greatest variance overall, because even a small amount of variance may be socially important if the behavior in question is considered important or even critical. In the theory of interpersonal behaviour, emotions, social factors (such as subjective norms in TRA), and habits are understood to be the main factors in the formation of personal intentions. TIB describes three levels to explain and predict people's behavior. The first level is formed by the personal beliefs, attitudes, social factors, and past experiences that condition the personal traits in the act. The second level describes how affects, cognitions, and social determinants along with personal normative beliefs affect intentions to behave in a particular way. At the third level, the possibility of a particular behavior is predicted by behavioral intentions, situational conditions, and past experiences. The main criticism of TIB is the high degree of complexity compared to TRA and TPB.



## 4.4 Technology Acceptance Model

The technology acceptance model (TAM) is derived from the TRA model and has further developed and refined it in several areas. The TAM is a model to capture the acceptance of technologies and was developed by Fred Davis already in 1985 (cf. Davis 1985). The model is intended to predict the likelihood of acceptance of new technologies within a group or organization (cf. Tang and Chen 2011).The model was originally developed to capture user acceptance of computers and information technologies. Davis generated the technology acceptance model (TAM) from the theory of reasoned action (TRA) (Fishbein and Ajzen 2001) and the theory of planned behaviour (TPB) (Ajzen 1991) (cf. Davis 1985). The TAM is composed of the acceptance variables "perceived benefits" (PB), "perceived ease of use" (PEOU), "attitude toward using" (ATT), "intention to use" (ITU), and "actual use of the system" (AUS).

In the technology acceptance model (◘ Fig. 4.1), external variables such as demographic factors influence both the perceived benefits (PB) and the perceived ease of use (PEOU) of a system by the user. Additionally, the perceived ease of use (PEOU) of a system can have a positive impact on the perceived benefits (PB) of a system. A system that is perceived to be user-friendly can make users comprehend the usefulness of a system. These two variables in turn influence users' attitudes towards the use (ATT) of systems (cf. Davis 1985; Song et al. 2011).

If the users show a positive attitude towards the application (ATT) of systems, this can contribute to the intended application (ITU) of the system. If the intention about the application (ITU) of a system is already present, this can lead to the actual application (AUS) of the system in the final step and finally complete and anchor the acceptance of the system, so to speak. Another direct relationship, according to Davis, is between the perceived benefits (PB) and the intended use (ITU) of a system. If the benefit of a system is perceived by the individual, this can lead to the intended use (ITU) of a system.

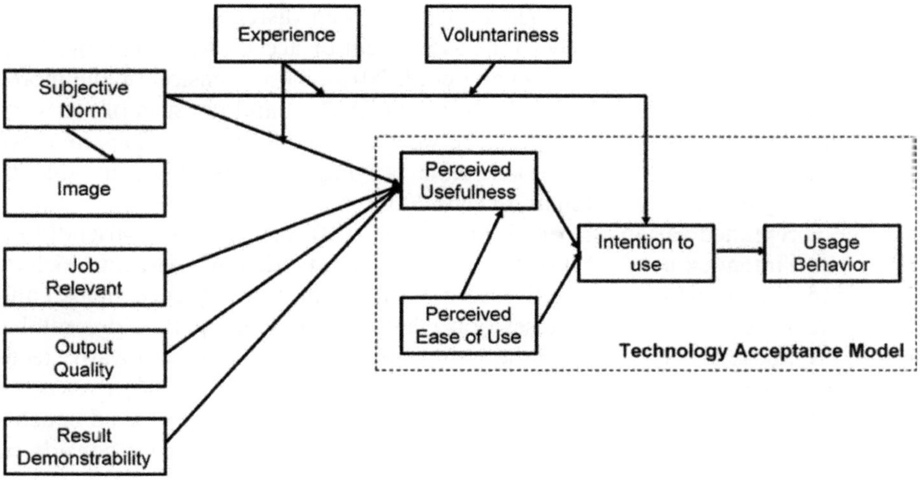


**Fig. 4.1** Technique acceptance model

**Background Information**
Perceived benefits

Perceived benefits (PB) is defined as "the degree to which a person believes that using a particular system will support his or her job performance" (cf. Davis 1985). According to Davis (1989), the PB variable is further subdivided into ten so-called items (cf. Davis 1985):

- quality of work
- control over work
- work more quickly
- critical to my job
- increase productivity
- job performance
- accomplish more work
- effectiveness
- makes job easier
- useful

The individual items are phrased as questions and could be rated using a seven-point Likert scale, from 1 (strongly disagree) to 7 (strongly agree). Davis assumes that systems with high perceived benefits (PB) by users is indicative of a positive relationship between use and performance delivered (cf. Davis 1985).

In contrast, perceived ease of use (PEOU), is the "degree to which a person believes that using a particular system is free of effort" (Davis 1985). According to Davis (1989), the PEOU is composed of the ten items: cubersome, ease of learning, frustrating, controllable, rigid and inflexible, ease of remembering, mental effort, understandable, effort to be skillful, and easy to use. These items are formulated and concretized in the form of a questionnaire (cf. Davis 1985).

### ▪ Extensions of the TAM

Over the years, the TAM of Venkatesh and Davis (2000) was extended, as factors necessary for the measurement and recording of acceptance of information technologies (e.g. social influences) had previously been disregarded. The model is intended to contribute positively to the assessment of acceptance in complex networks of social relationships (cf. Zhang et al. 2010). The extension of the model was named Technology Acceptance Model 2 (TAM 2) and consists of ten variables, each of which is subordinated to between two and four items. Each item can be answered using a seven-point Likert scale, ranging from 1 (strongly disagree) to 7 (strongly agree) (cf. Venkatesh and Davis 2000).



The acceptance variables: perceived benefits (PB), perceived user-friendliness (PUF) and intended use (ITU) of the TAM, were extended in TAM 2 to include social influence processes (subjective norm, voluntariness, experience, image) and instrumentalized cognitive processes (job relevance, outcome quality, presentable results). These ten variables target the actual application (AUS) of innovative technologies (cf. Venkatesh and Davis 2000).

Social influence processes and cognitive processes affect the perceived benefits (PB) of innovations. The processes influence whether an innovation is considered useful. Venkatesh and Davis (2000) point out in TAM 2 that acceptance variables can have both direct and indirect influence on perceived benefits (PB). For example, "experience" exerts both positive and negative influence on the relationship between a person's "subjective norm" and his or her perceived benefits (PB). Subjective norm can additionally influence the relationship between the variables "image" and perceived benefits (PB). The three variables perceived benefits (PB), perceived ease of use (PEOU) and subjective norm can have direct correlations with the intended use (ITU) of an innovation.

**Background Information**

Innovations and benefits

A perceived user-friendly (PEOU) innovation can have positive effects on the perceived benefits (PB) of an innovation. The relationship between the subjective norm of the users and the intended use (ITU) of an innovation is additionally influenced by the application-related experience and the voluntary nature of the use of an innovation (cf. Venkatesh and Davis 2000). According to Venkatesh and Davis, the social influence processes of TAM 2 reflect four interrelated factors that act on an individual to create the opportunity to accept or reject an innovation. "Social influences" are defined as "the influence of accepting information that comes from other sources of evidence of reality" (Venkatesh and Davis 2000). Social influences decrease significantly after the implementation of an innovation as both strengths and weaknesses become known through use and people gain increasing experience with the technology.

The first instance of the aforementioned social influence processes is the "subjective norm", which was adopted from the theory of reasoned action (TRA) and is defined as a "personal assessment of whether close people would approve or disapprove of a particular behaviour" (Fishbein and Ajzen 2001). Initially, the subjective norm was included in the development of the original TAM, but Davis et al. were unable to obtain significant correlations between the subjective norm and the acceptance variables (ITU, PB, PEOU) and thus excluded it at that time (cf. Venkatesh and Davis 2000).

In the second instance, the “experience” acquired through the use of the innovation can weaken the influence of the subjective norm. Users’ perceived uncertainties in using the innovation at the outset diminish through a longer period of use. Users recognise the strengths and weaknesses of an innovation and are thus no longer influenced by the views of others (subjective norm) (cf. Venkatesh and Davis 2000).

In the third instance, “voluntariness” is found as an independent variable in the technology acceptance model and is defined as “the extent to which potential users are willing to use a system without obligation” (Moore and Benbasat 1991).

The fourth instance is “image”, which has been adopted from “innovation diffusion theory” (IDT) and is defined by Moore and Benbasat (1991) as the “extent to which an innovation can raise an individual’s social status”.

**Background Information**

Variables of cognitive processes

The instrumentalized cognitive processes involved in the theory are composed of three variables:

- the “workplace relevance”, which is defined as “the extent to which a particular system is applicable to his or her workplace”;
- “quality of outcome”, which is defined as “the extent to which a system meets the objectives of the job and how beneficially those objectives can be met”; and
- the “presentable results”, which is defined as “accessibility to the presentation of the results that can be obtained by using an innovation” (Moore and Benbasat 1991; Venkatesh and Davis 2000).

Venkatesh and Bala picked up the gaps of acceptance of new technologies and their more efficient use, in the organizational level and managerial level respectively (Venkatesh and Bala 2008). This gap should be addressed by providing support in decision making in the use of information technologies. The aim is to improve the acceptance of information technologies. Later on, an extension of the TAM and TAM 2 was developed, which is consequently called Technology Acceptance Model 3 (TAM 3). TAM 3 is based on the acceptance variables of the original TAM (perceived usefulness, perceived ease of use, and intended use) and TAM 2 (experience, voluntariness, subjective norm, image, job relevance, outcome quality, demonstrable results). The model is complemented by the supercategories “anchor” and “adaptation”.

The theoretical framework of TAM 3 is based on TAM 2. In TAM 3 additional correlations and influences are shown: The influence of experience on anchors and adaptation, and the relationship between perceived ease of use (PEOU) and perceived benefits (PB). Outcome quality influences the relationship between job relevance and perceived benefits (PB) of a new technology.

The attached supercategories (anchors, adaptation) and their included variables are expected to have a direct impact on the perceived ease of use (PEOU) of new technologies. The first supercategory “anchors” includes the acceptance variables: Computer self-efficacy, perception of external control, computer anxiety, and computer enjoyment of play. The second supercategory adaptation includes: perceived enjoyment and objective fitness for use (cf. Venkatesh and Bala 2008).

4

**Definition**

The variables of the Anchor category are defined as follows:
- Computer self-efficacy – "Extent of ability to accomplish a specific task through the use of a computer" (Compeau and Higgins 1995);
- Perception of external control – "extent to which an individual believes that organizational and technical resources are available to support the use of a system" (Venkatesh et al. 2003);
- Computer anxiety – "Extent of an individual's concerns and fears about the possible use of computers" (Venkatesh 2000);
- Playfulness through computers – "Extent of cognitive spontaneity of interaction with microcomputers" (Webster and Martocchio 1992).

**Definition**

Adjustment variables

The variables mentioned in the category adaptation are defined as:
- perceived enjoyment – "active use of a particular system is seen as enjoyable, regardless of potential performance consequences of using a system" (Venkatesh 2000);
- Objective fitness for purpose – "comparison between systems based on their actual amount of work required to accomplish a particular task" (Venkatesh 2000).

The extension of the TAM generated by Tsai (2014) combines two theories, the "social cognitive theory" and the "social capital theory" with the TAM. Here, three variables from the "social capital theory" ("social trust" (ST), "institutional trust" (ITR), "social participation" (SPA)) and one variable from the "social cognitive theory" ("system self-efficacy" (SE)) were added to the three variables of the TAM ("perceived ease of use" (PEOU), "perceived benefits" (PB), "intended use" (ITU)). The seven variables of the model are subdivided into 17 items within a questionnaire when applied. The items of the questionnaire can be answered by a five-point Likert scale, from 1 ("strongly disagree") to 5 ("strongly agree").

**Background Information**

Influences on the perception of benefits

The theoretical framework of the model assumes that social trust (ST), institutional trust (ITR), social participation (SPA) and system self-efficacy (SE) influence the perceived ease of use (PEOU) of technical systems. It is hypothesized that institutional trust (ITR), social participation (SPA), and perceived ease of use (PEOU) influence the perceived benefits (PB) of technical systems. In the final instance, the two variables, perceived ease of use (PEOU) and perceived benefits (PB) should lead to the intended use (ITU) of technical systems (cf. Tsai 2014).

The seven variables just mentioned are defined as follows:
- "Social trust" (ST) refers to users' expectations of applications and their providers; users assume that they will act competently, fairly, transparently, and considerately.

- "Institutional trust" (ITR) is described as the individual's trust in the particular organization or institution.
- Social participation" (SPA) describes how actively a person participates in social leisure activities.
- System self-efficacy (SE) refers to a person's belief that he or she can apply certain technical systems.
- Perceived ease of use" (PEOU) describes the extent to which users perceive the use of technical systems as effortless.
- The "perceived benefits" (PB) is described as the extent of a positive management, a desirable improvement of the state, which is to be achieved by the application of the technical system.

The TAM offers great value for the study of adaptations of AI-supported systems and applications. The model assumes that acceptance is positively influenced by individual benefit recognition, which may well be the case in the context of artificial intelligence, since AI technologies are mainly used to support people in workflows and processes. In addition, the TAM is explicitly geared to work processes and work applications "on the job" and, when examining acceptance, focuses on the criteria of efficiency and relief as well as facilitation of work. In the vast majority of cases, AI applications aim to increase efficiency in processes and workflows and to make work easier by automating strenuous but at the same time monotonous tasks.

## 4.5 Diffusion of Innovations Theory

The theory of diffusion of innovation (DOI), developed by E.M. Rogers in 1962, is now one of the oldest social science theories. It originated in communication theory to explain how an idea or product gains momentum over time and spreads (or diffuses) throughout a particular society or social system. The result of this diffusion is that people adopt a new idea, behavior, or product as part of a social system. Adoption here means that a person does something different from what they did before (i.e., buy or use a new product, acquire and perform a new behavior). The key to adoption is that the person must perceive the idea, behavior, or product as new or innovative. Only in this way is diffusion possible (cf. Rogers 2003).

The adoption of a new idea, a new behaviour or a new product, i.e. an innovation of any kind, does not happen simultaneously in a social system. Rather, it is a process in which some people are more able to adopt the innovation than others. Diffusion of innovation theory describes that people who adopt an innovation early have different characteristics than people who adopt an innovation later. To specifically support or promote an innovation to a target group, it is important to understand the characteristics of the target group that help or hinder the adoption of the innovation. There are five established categories related to innovation adoption. Although the majority of the general population tends to fall into the middle categories, it is still necessary to understand the characteristics of the target groups. This is true for external audiences (customers) as well as internal audiences (employees). When promoting an innovation, there are different strategies to address the different target groups or categories.

Innovators – These are people who want to be the first to try innovation. They are daring and interested in new ideas. They are very willing to take risks and are often the first to come up with new ideas. Very little, if anything, needs to be done to appeal to this target group.

Early adopters – people who are considered opinion leaders. They enjoy leadership roles and embrace change opportunities. They are already aware of the need for change and therefore embrace new ideas. Strategies to appeal to this audience include how-to guides, tutorials, and likewise implementation fact sheets.

Early majority – These people are rarely leaders, but they still adopt new ideas earlier than the average user. Still, they usually need to see evidence that the innovation works before they are willing to adopt it for themselves as well. Strategies to appeal to this audience include success stories and evidence of the innovation's effectiveness.

Late majority – These people are skeptical of change and will not adopt an innovation until it has been tried by the majority. Strategies to target this group include information about how many other people have tried and successfully adopted the innovation.

Laggards – These people are bound by tradition and are very conservative. They are very skeptical of change and are the hardest group to convince. Strategies to appeal to this target group include statistics, fear appeals and social or economic pressure from people in the other target groups.

The stages in which an individual adopts an innovation and diffusion is achieved include awareness of the need for an innovation, the decision to adopt (or reject) the innovation, initial use of the innovation to test it, and continued use of the innovation. There are five main factors that influence the adoption of an innovation, and each of these factors is important to varying degrees in the five target groups.

- Relative advantage – The degree to which an innovation is considered superior to the idea, program, or product it replaces.
- Compatibility – How consistent the innovation is with the values, experiences and needs of potential users and adopters?
- Complexity – How difficult it is to understand and/or use the innovation?
- Trialability – The extent to which the innovation can be tested or tried before a commitment to adoption is made.
- Observability – The extent to which the innovation delivers perceptible and quantifiable results.

**Background Information**

Criticism of the DOI

There are several limitations and criticisms of the diffusion of innovation theory:

- Much of the evidence for this theory, including target groups or categories, comes from more or less classical consumer markets. The extent to which the theory can also be applied to regulated markets is uncertain. The same applies to the applicability to innovations in organisations and companies.
- Theory does not promote a participatory approach.
- It works better with adopting behaviors than with stopping or preventing behaviors.
- It does not take into account an individual's resources or social support to adopt the new behavior (or innovation).

## 4.6 Other Acceptance Theories

- **Percieved Characteristics of Innovation Theory (PCIT)**

This model extends the diffusion of innovation theory by seeking to account for three additional characteristics: image, voluntariness and behavior. Accordingly, behavior is influenced by the perception of voluntariness, which affects actual behavior. The theory describes that adoption rate and perception of voluntariness are closely positively related to each other and thus adoption rate can be increased. Furthermore, this perceptibility is composed of two sub-features: The visibility and the detectability of an outcome. Also in PCI theory, voluntariness influences the users' decision to reject or accept an innovation (cf. Hameed et al. 2012).

- **Social Cognitive Theory (SCT)**

Inspired by social psychology, social cognitive theory was developed based on three main factors: behavior, personality, and environment, which interact bidirectionally to predict both group and individual behavior. In addition, the theory aims to identify methods that can change and modify behavior (see Rana and Dwivedi 2015). In the SCT model, the behavioral factor focuses mainly on issues of use, performance, and adoption. The personal factor includes cognitive and demographic aspects that characterize a person. Social cognitive theory describes an inseparable triangular structure where all three factors influence and determine each other. The SCT model is applied to evaluate the use of information technology by using some constructs such as self-efficacy, outcome expectations, performance, anxiety, affect, and outcome expectations.

- **Motivational Model (MM)**

Basically, according to the motivational model, system use is determined by two factors: intrinsic motivation and extrinsic motivation. Extrinsic motivation is defined as the perception that users want to perform an activity because it helps to achieve outcomes of value to the person that are different from the activity itself being performed, such as an improved work position. Intrinsic motivation is defined as the perception that people perform an activity without having or seeking a benefit that is distinct from the process of performing the activity itself. In this regard, Davis et al. (1992) postulate that perceived benefits should be considered as an extrinsic motivation and perceived enjoyment as an intrinsic motivation. In general, the quality of a (work) outcome and perceived ease of use affect perceived enjoyment and perceived usefulness. Furthermore, they elaborated the importance of usability as a driver of motivation, as well as the influence of outcome quality on the perceived benefits of an activity and thus motivation. Therefore, outcome quality and perceived ease of use indirectly influence the adoption of technological innovations through perceived benefits and perceived advantage.

- **Uses and Gratification Theory (UGT)**

This model attempts to analyze the reason for using and participating in certain communication and work technologies. The main focus of uses and gratification is on the social and psychological aspects of users' consumption and their related pursuit of motivation and satisfaction. The UGT includes three main aspects: motivation, behavioral uses, and satisfactions or contentment. Motivation refers to the overall dispositions that influence people's actions for their needs (see Chen et al. 2015). Behavioral use refers to "patterns of exposure to use (such as amount of use, duration of use, and type of use)" (cf. Chen et al. 2015). The Uses and Gratification Theory is an established framework that is primarily applied to all types of media compared to other models such as TPB and DOI. However, the U&G model is not only used for communication media but is also related to media for playing and in the work process.



#### ▪ Model of PC Utilization (MPCU)

The model of PC usage belongs to the methods of predicting individual acceptance and personal computer (PC) usage. The MPCU model considers the actual behavior (PC usage) and assumes that this usage is also basically intentional. In addition, habits are not included in the model because habits are assumed to have a tautological relationship to actual PC use among people.[1] Specifically, the MPCU model examines the direct influences of experienced use effect, long-term perceived consequences of consumption or use, social influences, complexity of use, and fit with one's job as factors in PC use behavior. Research findings confirm that fit to one's job, social factors, long-term consequences, and complexity have a strong influence on PC use (see Chang 2015).

#### ▪ Unified Theory of Acceptance and Use of Technology (UTAUT)

Venkatesh et al. (2003) compared the similarities and differences between the models previously described here, all of which had their origins in sociology, psychology and communication. Explicitly these are technology acceptance model, Theory of Reasoned Action, combined TAM and TPB, theory of planned behaviour, model of PC utilization, diffusion of innovation, motivational model and social cognitive theory. The resulting unified theory of acceptance and use of technology (UTAUT) identified four conditions of acceptance of technological systems. They were developed by adapting the 14 initial constructs from acceptance theories (cf. Venkatesh et al. 2003). The significant criteria are effort expectancy, performance expectancy, social influence, and facilitating conditions. In addition, four significant moderating variables were identified: Gender, experience, age, and voluntariness of use.

#### ▪ Compatibility UTAUT (C-UTAUT)

Bouten (2008) integrated the compatibility beliefs developed by Karahanna et al. (2006) into the UTAUT model developed by Venkatesh and Morris to improve the explanatory power of the UTAUT model. They aimed to gain a deeper understanding of how the cognitive phenomena of the UTAUT model are formed by identifying and testing new frameworks. As the theory involved investigating the

1 Whether this tautological relationship is exclusively typical for PC use can be questioned.

relationship between compatibility beliefs and behavioural perceptions, the measurement of actual usage behaviour was not considered to be of importance. In addition, this was a cross-sectional study where measuring behavioral intention rather than usage behavior circumvented the potential problem of retrospective analysis. Because it was a cross-sectional study and did not test different time periods, the relationships proposed by Venkatesh and Morris in terms of experience could not ultimately be demonstrated and validated.

**Background Information**

Technology acceptance and AI implementation

After the presentation and critical analysis of the theories of acceptance and adoption of technologies and technical innovations, the TAM can be considered the most appropriate for the issues raised in this research. The most important points here are the integration of explicit work aspects in the model, the orientation towards the individual, the integration of self-efficacy aspects in the model and the integration of motivational aspects in the model. It is precisely these motivational aspects, or rather even the theoretical and scientific foundations of motivation itself and the so-called self determination theory associated with it, that are now also the focus of the following chapter.

## Literature

Ajzen, I. "The Theory of Planned Behavior," Organizational Behavior and Human Decision Processes (50:2), 1991, pp. 179–211

Bouten, M.P.: Compatibility and Technology Acceptance: Consolidating, Validating and Extending Concep, in Faculty of Economics and Business Administration, Maastricht 2008

Chang, S.-S.: Exploration of usage behavioral model construction for university library electronic resources. The Electronic Library.33(2)(2015)292–307

Chen, C.D.; Huang, C.K.; Ku, E.C.S..: User's adoption of mobile o2o applications: perspectives of the uses and gratifications paradigm and service dominant logic. PACIS 2015

Compeau, D.R.; Higgins, C.A.: Computer self-efficacy: Development of a measure and initial test', Management Information Systems Research Center (MIS) Quarterly, vol. 19, no. 2/1995, pp: 189–211, p.192

Davis, F.D.: A Technology Acceptance Model for empirically testing new end-user information systems; theory and results, Massachusetts Institute of Technology, pp: 1–291, Massachusetts 1985, S.82; S.329

Davis, F.D.: Perceived usefulness, perceived ease of use, and user acceptance of information technology. In: MIS Quarterly, 9 (1989) S.319–340

Davis, F.D.; Bagozzi, R.P.; Warshaw, P.R.: Extrinsic and intrinsic motivation to use computers in the workplace. Journal of Applied Social Psychology. 22 (1992) 1111–1132

Fishbein, M.; Ajzen, I.: Belief, attitude, intention and behavior: An introduction to theory and research, MA: Addison-Wesley, 1975; M.K. Chang, W. Cheung, Determinants of the intention to use Internet/WWW at work: a confirmatory study. Information & Management. 39(2001)1–14, S.302

Hameed, M.A.; Counsell, S.; Swift, S.: A conceptual model for the process of IT innovation adoption in organizations. Journal of Engineering and Technology Management.29(3)(2012)358–390

Karahanna, E.; Agarwal, R.; Angst, C.M.: Reconceptualizing compatibility beliefs in technology acceptance research. MIS Quarterly, 30(4)/2006, S.781–804

Kuo, B.C.; Roldan-Bau, A.; Lowinger, R.: Psychological help seeking among latin american immigrants in Canada: Testing a culturally expanded model of the theory of reasoned action using path analysis, International Journal for the advancement of counselling 37(2), 2015, S.179–179

Mathieson, K.: Predicting user intentions: comparing the technology acceptance model with the theory of planned behavior. Information Systems Research. 2(3) (1991) 173–191.

Moore, G.C.; Benbasat, I.: Development of an instrument to measure the perceptions of adopting an information technology innovation, Information Systems Research, vol. 2, no. 3/1991, pp: 192–222, p.195; p.203

Rana, N.P.; Dwivedi, Y.K.: Citizen's adoption of an e-government system: Validating extended social cognitive theory (SCT). Government Information Quarterly. 32(2)(2015)172–181

Rogers, E.: Diffusion of Innovations, New York 2003

Simon, B.: Wissensmedien im Bildungssektor. Eine Akzeptanzuntersuchung an Hochschulen, Wien 2001

Song, L.; Park, B.; Oh, K.M.: Analysis of the technology acceptance model in examining hospital nurses` behavioral intentions toward the use of bar code medication administration', Computers, Informatics, Nursing (CIN), vol. 33, no.4/2011, pp: 157–165

Taherdoost, H., S. Sahibuddin, and N. Jalaliyoon, Smart Card Security; Technology and Adoption. International Journal of Security, 2011a. 5(2): p. 74–84

Taherdoost, H.; Namayandeh, M.; Jalaliyoon, N.: Information Security and Ethics in Educational Context: Propose a Conceptual Framework to Examine Their Impact. International Journal of Computer Science and Information Security. 9(1)(2011b)134–138

Tang, DP & Chen, LJ 2011, 'A review of the evolution of research on information technology acceptance model', Business Management and Electronic Information (BMEI), 2011 International Conference on 13–15 May 2011 in Guangzhou, China, pp: 588–591, https://doi.org/10.1109/ICBMEI.2011.5917980

Tsai, C.H.: Integrating social capital theory, social cognitive theory, and the technology acceptance model to explore a behavioral model of telehealth systems', International Journal of Environmental Research and Public Health, vol. 11, no. 5/2014, pp: 4905–4925

Venkatesh, V.: Determinants of perceived ease of use: Integrating perceived behavioral control, computer anxiety and enjoyment into the technology acceptance model, Information Systems Research, vol. 11, no. 4/2000, pp: 342–365, p.349; p.351

Venkatesh, V.; Bala, H.: Technology Acceptance Model 3 and a research agenda on interventions, Decision Sciences, vol. 39, no. 2/2008, pp: 273–315

Venkatesh, V.; Davis, F.D.: A theoretical extension of the Technology Acceptance Model: Four longitudinal field studies', Management Science, vol. 46/2000, no. 2, pp: 186–204, S.190

Venkatesh, V.; Morris, M.G.; Davis, G.B.; Davis, F.D.: User acceptance of information technology: Toward a unified view', Management Information Systems Research Center (MIS) Quarterly, vol. 27, no. 3/2003, pp: 425–478, p.30

Webster, J.; Martocchio, J.J. : Microcomputer playfulness: Development of a measure with workplace implications, Management Information Systems Research Center (MIS) Quarterly, vol. 16, no. 2/1992, pp: 201–226, p.204

Zhang, H.; Cocosila, M.; Archer, N.: Factors of adoption of mobile information technology by homecare nurses: A technology acceptance model 2 approach, Computers, Informatics, Nursing (CIN), vol. 28, no.1/2010, pp: 49–56.

# Basic Principles of Motivation

Contents




A. Moring, *AI on The Job*,
https://doi.org/10.1007/978-3-662-64005-0_5

Motivation is the key to success. This is true for all personal goals and plans; it is also true for the success of companies. Motivated employees are more productive, more agile and more innovative. Motivation is determined by three basic principles. These will be presented and analyzed here. The focus of the analysis is on the question of how these basic principles of motivation relate to the ways in which artificial intelligence functions and works, as described in the previous chapter. Since we find interaction between humans and machines practically everywhere in companies, and more and more "intelligent" machines in the future, these relationships are of particular importance. Motivation therefore depends strongly on the use of the technology and on the embedding of the technology in the processes, organisation and management in the company.



As preparation and basis for the following considerations, three of the basic motivation theories shall be presented first. These are achievement motivation, connection motivation and power motivation. This is intended to provide an initial basic understanding of why and how people can be motivated and motivate themselves. This presentation and description will then be deepened with the presentation and explanation of the so-called self determination theory. This theory builds on the three types of motivation mentioned above and also includes other internal and external factors of people and their environment in order to explain and predict motivation. In particular, work environments play a role here, which are important in view of the focus of this study. Subsequently, the so-called jobs demands-resources model is presented. This model also describes framework conditions and prerequisites for motivation (and demotivation), in this case specifically related to the work context defined by the requirements and resources of a specific task in which people move. In these sections, the general explanation of motivation in the actions and work of people is thus to be given according to the current and general state of science and research.

## 5.1 Performance Motivation

Behaviour is considered to be achievement-motivated if it is directed towards the attainment of a standard of quality ("competition with some standard of excellence") (cf. McClelland et al. 1953), i.e. one strives to master a task, to do something particularly well, to surpass oneself or also to prove oneself in competition with others, as is already clear in Murray's description of the need for achievement (1938). Achievement-motivated behaviour can be observed in a wide variety of areas of life, wherever people set themselves challenges in which they can prove themselves or fail. Central, moreover, is the assumption that the incentive for action lies exclusively in the enjoyment of the task-related activity itself (cf. Atkinson 1957) ("thrill of accomplishment") and/or in the self-evaluative emotions in the event of success (satisfaction, pride) or failure (shame, dejection). Diligence, dogged perseverance, and determination are colloquial attributes of an "achievement-motivated person." However, if they are shown exclusively to impress others or even to obtain a material reward, they are by no means indicators of achievement motivation in the narrower motivational-psychological sense. Thus, it is not the so-called "surface features" of the action that matter, but the affective experience, as is made clear in a definition of achievement motive by Schultheiss (cf. Schultheiss 2008). He sees the core of the achievement motive in deriving affective satisfaction from the self-directed mastery of performance requirements (cf. Schultheiss 2008).

**Background Information**
Meaning of "motives"

The thematic apperception test (TAT) by Morgan and Murray (1938) is used to measure achievement motivation. It is based on the idea that fantasies tell us something about one's own wishes and needs, i.e. one's "motives". Accordingly, in this so-called projective test, subjects are asked to formulate fantasy stories about ambiguous pictures. When the TAT became available as a measure of achievement motive, it had to be shown that the achievement motive score allowed prediction of relevant behavior; this is referred to as predictive validity. A large number of studies were conducted to validate the TAT (cf. Heckhausen et al. 1985), whereby the experimental designs were relatively simple: Subjects' achievement motivation scores were correlated with their performance in tasks requiring effort, concentration, and perseverance (e.g., solving arithmetic problems). Indeed, in these experimental tasks, subjects with a strong achievement motive performed better than those with a weak achievement motive. This finding was interpreted in such a way that the former enjoyed the challenge more, were more absorbed in the task itself, and experienced greater pleasure and satisfaction in (partial) successes, which motivated them to persevere and work thoroughly.

If the achievement motive predicted achievement behavior, it was reasonable to assume that individuals with a strong achievement motive would achieve more in school and work than those with a weak achievement motive, even though far more complex influences on the occurrence of achievement would be expected for these situations. Indeed, McClelland and Franz (1992) report a respectable correlation between achievement motive measured at age 31 and the earnings of employed men 10 years later. Andrews (1967), in a field study, analyzed the relationship between achievement motive and occupational position in a company where promotions were made on the merit principle and a company where career advancement was made on the seniority principle. In the former company, high levels of achievement motive were associated with a higher job position and higher income. In the second company, achievement motive and achieved occupational status were not correlated. Since achievement motive scores had been collected 2–4 years prior to the collection of the occupational achievement measure, the alternative explanation that occupational position led to motive enhancement and not vice versa can be ruled out. Andrews' study is noteworthy in that it took into account the motivational stimulus content of the situation (company performance ethos) and thus took seriously the long postulated person-environment interaction in predicting behavior. The author used the term "congruence between individual motive scores and dominant firm orientation" (Andrews 1967) - congruence between the individual's motive and the motivational stimuli of the situation - a theoretical concept that is receiving much attention again today.

#### ▪ The Risk Choice Model

Under John W. Atkinson, a second very influential school of achievement motivation research developed. His publication "Motivational determinants of risk-taking behavior" from 1957 became one of the most cited psychological articles. In it, Atkinson presents a mathematically formalised theory of achievement motivation, the name of which, “risk-choice model”, already suggests that it deals with choice decisions under uncertainty. The central question in Atkinson’s model is: Which task does a person choose when faced with tasks of varying difficulty? This question arises frequently in everyday life. The choice of task is of great importance because it ultimately determines the learning experiences a person has and thus also the extent to which he or she develops his or her competencies. Underdemanding or overdemanding tasks do not contribute to an increase in learning and prevent the experience of having achieved success through one’s own efforts - an experience that is very important from the point of view of motivation psychology because it strengthens the experience of self-efficacy (cf. Bandura 1977; Meyer 1984).

Compared to the research presented so far on the achievement motive, Atkinson’s approach brings several striking innovations:

- Atkinson differentiates the achievement motive construct and distinguishes two motive components with the “success motive” (motive to achieve success) and the “failure motive” (motive to avoid failure).
- To predict behavior, an environmental component (task difficulty and attractiveness) is considered in addition to the person (achievement motive) (analysis of person-environment interaction).
- The choice decision is viewed as a function of the (in)attractiveness (value) of success or failure and the probability of their occurrence (expectation). Thus, the risk-choice model is one of the widely used and influential expectancy-value theories in psychology and economics.

So what does it depend on whether a person chooses an undemanding, a challenging, or even a completely overwhelming task? According to Atkinson (1957), three theoretical constructs are needed for prediction: (1) the individual motive, (2) the subjective expectancy, and (3) the incentive.

Atkinson defines a motive under the term “motive construct“as a “disposition to strive for a certain kind of satisfaction” (1957); the affective character of the motive is thus emphasised here. Further, the two motive components success motive (M(e); achievement motive) and failure motive (M(m); motive to avoid failure) are distinguished. The affective core of the achievement motive is pride (“pride in accomplishment”), that of the failure motive is shame (“shame and humiliation as a consequence of failure”) (cf. Atkinson 1957). Atkinson’s model is simplified in that the achievement motive and the anticipated self-evaluative emotions are regarded as the sole drivers of task choice and performance behaviour, and no other motives (e.g. to be liked by others) or goals (e.g. to gain an economic advantage) play a role. The second relevant construct is the expectation of the extent to which one will succeed or fail in the task. It results from a person’s previous experiences with similar tasks or from the dispositional self-concept of one’s own talent (cf. Meyer 1984; Dickhäuser 2006), but can also be induced situationally by normative information or trial runs with actually easy or difficult tasks. The probability of success is expressed on a scale from 0 (success will certainly not occur, 0% probability of success) to 1 (success will certainly occur, 100% probability of success).

#### ■ The Decisive Role of the "Incentive"

Initially, one might assume that people will only choose tasks in which they are very likely to succeed. However, Atkinson's model of performance is mainly about positive self-evaluation. This is where the third determinant, incentive, comes in. Successfully completing a simple task does not bring the desired pride in one's performance. The more difficult the task was, the higher the pleasure of success. Thus, an inverse-linear relationship is assumed between the subjective probability of success (We) and the incentive for success (Ae). Another aspect: In a performance situation, typically two tendencies are stimulated simultaneously, since on the one hand one strives for success (Te; seeking success tendency; "motivation to achieve"), on the other hand one tries to avoid failure (Tm; avoiding failure tendency; "motivation to avoid failure"). These two tendencies have to be combined to form the so-called resultant motivation tendency (Tr), because "the act which is performed among a set of alternatives is the act for which the resultant motivation is most positive" (Atkinson 1958).

How can success and failure motivation be identified? Success-motivated individuals approach performance tasks with optimism and openness, often even explicitly expressing the confidence that "it will work out", while failure-motivated individuals are plagued by fears and doubts because they are more likely to face failure than success. For success-motivated individuals, tasks of moderate difficulty should be particularly motivating, while very easy and very difficult tasks should be hardly motivating at all. For failure-motivated individuals, while all performance tasks are daunting, very easy and very difficult tasks are relatively the least daunting. However, when failure-motivated individuals must choose a task and cannot avoid it, they will prefer very easy or very difficult tasks.

Further research on the risk-choice model has, for example, addressed the question of the motivational dependence of the incentive or whether affect maximization (pride about one's performance) rather than information gain (orientation as to how good one really is) is really the driving force behind task choice (cf. Heckhausen et al. 1985; Heckhausen and Heckhausen 2018). There have also been attempts to apply the risk choice model to task choice relevant in everyday life. For example, Isaacson was able to show (1964) that success-motivated individuals were more likely to choose a study program of moderate difficulty than a very easy or very difficult one; again, no clear pattern of results was evident for failure-motivated students. Mahone's (1960) findings are also considered convincing: 75% of the success-motivated students studied indicated a realistic career aspiration, whereas this was true for only 39% of the failure-motivated students; they had in mind occupations which, according to expert assessment, were to be regarded as under- or over-challenging in relation to their abilities.

#### ■ Subjective Attributions and Performance Outcomes

Weiner's attributional theory of achievement motivation focuses on subjective attributions of causes for achievement results and thus on cognitive processes (cf. Weiner et al. 1971). The beginning of this theoretical tradition dates back to the 1950s and 1960s and can be traced back to Fritz Heider and Harold Kelley, who were the first to recognize the significance of causal thinking and make it the object of scientific psychological analysis (cf. Heider 1958; Kelley 1967). The starting point of attribution theory is that people are not satisfied with merely registering events in their environment; rather, they strive to explain them and to find the causes for these events. Such explanations of causes are called attributions. They fulfil an important function for the acting individual: order can be brought into the complex sequence of events, and one can adapt one's own behaviour to the requirements of the environment and thus gain control over it. Meaning: Only when I know which cause is responsible for an event, I can act accordingly. In connection with the analysis of cause attributions, two different lines of research can be found. One considers on the basis of which information people arrive at certain cause attributions (e.g. Kelley's covariation principle of 1967). These are attribution theories in the narrower sense. Approaches which, on the other hand, address the consequences of attributions on experience and behaviour are referred to as attributional theories. The core message of the attributional theory of achievement motivation is that the two determinants of achievement behavior already mentioned in the risk-choice model, "affective self-evaluation" and "expectancy," depend on the type of cause attribution. Although myriad possible causes of success and failure exist, four factors are commonly cited: ability, effort/commitment, task difficulty, and chance (luck/poverty), which can also be confirmed in cultural comparisons (cf. Schuster et al. 1989). Ultimately, our thoughts influence how we feel and how we act. Weiner et al. (1971) arranged attributions in a two-dimensional scheme and distinguished them according to whether they are internal to the person (internal) or external to the person (environment, external) on the one hand, and whether they are stable or variable over time on the other.



Later, Weiner (1979) added the third dimension of controllability, but this is not central to the core theoretical proposition. The "internality/externality" dimension is supposed to determine the affective consequences of a performance event, whereas the "stability/instability" dimension is supposed to influence how one expects to perform in future performance situations. Weiner and others postulate that it is primarily internally attributed events that are affect-relevant, in both positive and negative cases. The assumptions about the stability dimension are: If a performance outcome is explained by a stable causal factor, then the expectation of success decreases after failure, and increases after success. However, if variable factors are held responsible for the outcome, then one observes constant or only slightly increasing expectations of success after success and constant or slightly decreasing expectations of success after failure. The attributional theory of achievement motivation makes predictions about the antecedent conditions of subjective probability of success and affective experience (expectancy and value components). This provides an ideal link to the risk-choice model, especially since it had been discovered that success-motivated and failure-motivated individuals differ in their attributional habits (the so-called attributional style) (cf. Stiensmeier-Pelster 1988; Stiensmeier-Pelster et al. 1994). Success-motivated individuals habitually attribute success to their own ability (stable, internal), whereas failures are attributed by this group of individuals to variable factors (e.g. lack of effort, bad luck). In the case of success, performance situations offer them the opportunity for positive self-assessment; in the case of failure, they can remain confident that things will go better next time. Overall, this attribution pattern is motivationally favorable. In comparison, the attribution habits of those motivated to fail are much less favourable: they explain failure with a lack of ability and attribute their own successes to fortunate circumstances or the ease of the task. The self-assessment and success expectation balance are correspondingly unfavourable: successes do not have an affective effect; after all, it is external circumstances that have helped one to succeed, so why should one be proud of oneself? Things look even bleaker in the case of failures: Attribution to a stable internal factor is associated with negative self-evaluative reactions and declining expectations of success. Over time, those motivated by failure can develop the syndrome of "learned helplessness", because failure is experienced by the person concerned as uncontrollable, which in the long term is associated with resignation and depressive mood (cf. Stiensmeier-Pelster 1988).

## 5.2 Connection Motivation

In all phases of their lives, people strive for satisfying interpersonal relationships in old and new acquaintances, in friendships, in partnerships and in the family (cf. Baumeister and Leary 1995). Feeling socially included is considered an important basic human need, the satisfaction of which has positive consequences for one's well-being and physical well-being, and the frustration of which has negative consequences (cf. Deci 1985; Deci and Ryan 2000).When people are asked what are particularly significant or meaningful goals in their lives, they often mention themes that revolve around social relationships. Motivational psychology postulates a separate motive for the pursuit of interpersonally satisfying relationships: the connection motive.

**Background Information**

Connection as life insurance

The bond to close reference persons such as parents, children and partners as well as the ability to join together in social groups and to maintain harmony here for the benefit of the cohesion and functioning of the group was an important condition for survival at all times of humanity. For example, humans were dependent on food procurement activities that were only possible in groups (in most cases this involved hunting). In addition, there was the threat of animals. The long gestation period in relation to other creatures, during which mothers as well as children are relatively defenceless against enemies, and the long childhood, during which skills necessary for survival are only available to a limited extent, describe only a few examples of the vulnerability of the individual. Social bonds within (filial and parental love) and outside one's own family (communities of purpose, friendships) are thus necessary in evolutionary biology and form the core of the connection motive (cf. Bischof-Köhler 1985).

The phylogenetic basis of the attachment motif is also at the core of Bowlby's (1958) attachment theory approach. According to this, mothers and children are phylogenetically predisposed to respond to each other with emotional and physical affection and to feel sadness and fear when separated. While babies react positively (smiling) to strangers up to about the sixth month of life, fear of strangers is often observed between the seventh and ninth month. This fear, also known as "strangeness," ranges from reticence to intense fear and can persist beyond the first year of life. Hope and fear in the context of social contact are thus phylogenetically based "expectancy emotions." These are emotions that are not tied to a current situation but arise from the expectation of the occurrence of a future event, which also play a crucial role in the later formation of the attachment motive. According to Ainsworth et al. (1978), attachment quality differs between mothers and their children. This can be described in terms of attachment types that are quite stable over time and also relevant for later social relationships in adulthood. The attachment types are determined by means of the "stranger situation" paradigm, in which the attachment figure - usually the mother - leaves her infant (1–1.5 years) alone with the experimenter. The children's behavior at separation and reunion is observed and evaluated. The following four attachment types can be distinguished: secure attachment style (separation from mother triggers negative feelings in the child, but she remains calm and shows joy upon her return), insecure-avoidant attachment style (child seems unimpressed by the separation and ignores mother upon her return), insecure-ambivalent attachment style (child seems desperate when separated, shows contradictory behaviour from clinging to aggressive-rejecting when returned) and disorganised attachment style (conspicuous behaviour in severely neglected children, no reaction to caregiver, stereotypical behaviour such as rocking).



■ **Early Learning Experiences with Long-Lasting Effects**

Early learning experiences are considered to be a significant factor for the formation of the attachment types. For example, the mother's sensitive response to the child's nonverbal signals is considered central to a secure attachment style. Although it is intuitively obvious that attachment experiences contribute to the formation of hope-for-attachment and fear-of-rejection, no studies exist that empirically test this relationship. There are also few studies that directly analyze the development of the connection motive. McClelland and Boyatzis (1982) cite findings from longitudinal studies that the attachment motive measured in adulthood correlates with parenting style (use of affirming parenting techniques such as praise). Contrary to this, however, one finding also indicates that the connection motive has its roots in fear of rejection. Thus, the best predictor of high attachment motive among 31-year-old adults was ignoring crying by the mother in early childhood.

Social relationships are a source of happiness, satisfaction and well-being. However, the other side of the coin is that they are also one of the most powerful sources of unhappiness, dissatisfaction and ill-being. Rejections and breakups are common reasons for seeking counseling or psychotherapy. Social rejection causes a whole range of negative emotional reactions such as offending, anxiety, sadness and depression. In addition to emotions, it also impairs cognitive processes and self-regulation. That rejection literally "hurts" is explained by a study by Eisenberger and others (2003). Using functional magnetic resonance imaging (fMRI), they found that social exclusion engages a midbrain area (anterior cingulate gyrus) that also becomes active during physical pain. DeWall and others (2010) also argue that physical pain and "social pain" rely on similar neural mechanisms. In their experiments, they tested whether a commonly used painkiller (acetaminophen) also alleviated the negative effects of social rejection. Using functional magnetic resonance imaging, they found that paracetamol indeed decreased neuronal activity in those brain regions associated with "social pain" (and with the affective component of physical pain) (dorsal anterior cingulate cortex, anterior insula).

**Background Information**
Hope and fear
As with the achievement motive and the power motive described below, a distinction is made between a hope and a fear component in the connection motive. While the "hope of connection" represents a generalised expectation of success in social relationships and is geared towards establishing social contacts, the "fear of rejection", on the other hand, as a generalised expectation of failure in social relationships, inhibits an inappropriate approach to other people. The motive components work in opposite directions and thereby regulate each other in the sense of an optimal closeness and distance to other people. When in the literature and further on in this study "hope-for-connection-motivated" and "fear-of-rejection-motivated" are written, this does not mean an either-or, but a relative predominance of one of the two components.

According to Mehrabian and Ksionsky (1974), individuals with "hope of connection" differ from individuals with "fear of rejection" in a whole range of characteristics. "Hope of connection" motivated individuals, for example, are characterized by the following features: They judge other persons more positively. They think other persons are more like themselves. They report liking others more and they are liked more by others. "Fear of rejection" motivators, for example, tend to interpret ambiguous signals in social situations as rejection (cf. Sokolowksi and Schmalt 1996). They do not behave particularly skillfully in social situations and feel more unpopular and lonely. The partial excessive demands in social situations are transferred to their social interaction partners (cf. Mehrabian and Ksionsky 1974).

The open and positive attention shown by "Hope to Connect" motivated individuals towards others has a contagious effect on them and often leads to a relaxed social atmosphere that fulfils the connection motive. "Hope to connect" motivated individuals are strengthened in their confidence that they can make positive social contacts and will continue to behave in a similarly socially adept manner in the future. In this cycle, hope stabilizes. The principle of self-affirming motive also applies, of course, to "fear of rejection" motivators. The tendency to quickly detect rejection signals in social situations inevitably leads to an uncertain, cautious, or even fearful approach. The social interaction partners sense the (on)tension and feel uncomfortable in the social atmosphere and precisely do not send signals that are almost urgently desired in this sense and that clearly indicate social acceptance. This ambiguity is in turn interpreted to the disadvantage of the quality of the relationship by those motivated by "fear of rejection".

Here the cycle is a vicious circle that stabilizes fear. Fear-motivated individuals tend to regulate their behavior through avoidance goals, whereas hope-motivated individuals tend to have approach goals. Gable (2006) supports the theoretical assumption that hope and fear, and the approach and avoidance goals associated with them, lead to the desired positive and feared negative consequences, respectively, in the connection context. She found in research that students who pursued social approach goals such as "make new friends" reported less loneliness and greater satisfaction with social relationships, whereas students who pursued social avoidance goals such as "avoid fighting with my boyfriend" felt more lonely and experienced greater relationship insecurity.

Connection-motivated students perform better when the performance situation contains connection-themed incentives. For example, they achieved better grades with sympathetic and likewise connection-motivated teachers (cf. McKeachie 1961), achieved the best work results when they worked in a group rather than alone (cf. French 1958a), and produced the best athletic performance when they competed for their team rather than individually (cf. Sorrentino and Sheppard 1978). When connection-motivated individuals are allowed to choose between work partners who are competent but not particularly likeable and those who are likeable but not particularly competent, they are more likely to choose the latter than are low connection-motivated individuals (cf. French 1958b). They thus prefer connection incentives that would result from working with a likeable colleague to better performance outcomes. Individuals with strong connection motives perform well on tasks that require cooperation and perform poorly when competition is required (cf. Koestner et al. 1992). In hierarchical organizations, high connection motivators are rarely found in managerial positions, but they are found in organizations with flat hierarchies, where harmonious interactions of group processes are more important (cf. Litwin and Siebrecht 1967).



## 5.3 Power Motivation

Schultheiss (2008) describes the power motive as the tendency to derive satisfaction from exerting physical, mental, or emotional influence over others. Earlier power motive definitions also focus on influencing and controlling others. Thus, according to Lewin (1951), power refers to another person on whom influence is exerted, the power of person 1 over person 2. Importantly, the positive feeling of strength associated with the exercise of power is considered the actual motivational goal (cf. McClelland 1985). People act because achieving their (power) goals is associated with feelings of control and self-efficacy, which in turn reinforces successful power-related behavior. Murray identified the need for dominance as an important basic psychological need as early as 1938 in his motive classification approach. He paraphrases it as "to influence or control others. To persuade, prohibit, dictate. To lead and direct. To restrain. To organize the behavior of a group" (Murray 1938).

**Background Information**

Experiencing power and strength

But how does one succeed in exerting influence on others in order to ultimately be able to experience a feeling of strength? According to French and Raven, the prerequisite for this is resource superiority over other people. French and Raven have categorized these resources into six sources of power (cf. French and Raven 1959):

- Reward and punishment power: Being able to reward or punish others for their behavior (e.g., teachers giving grades, supervisors sanctioning).
- Legitimate power: A person may legitimately exercise power against the will of another person on the basis of the norms or rules of a society (arrests by the police, sanctions by superiors for poor work performance).
- Role model power: Role models also exercise power in the sense that they cause others to become like them.

- Expert power: Expertise is another source of power where others rely on the knowledge or skills of another person. An example of expert power is medical health recommendations, which have more influence on behaviour change than, for example, the advice of an acquaintance.
- Information power: The source of power here is information about the persons to be influenced and the possibility of using this information to the advantage or disadvantage of these persons (e.g. strategic information play at the workplace or even blackmail).

While further theoretical considerations and empirical studies of sources of power show that the mere perceived possession of sources of power-without exercising it-is capable of satisfying the power motive, it also shows that the possession of sources of power, such as the ability to control others' resources, spurs power-related actions.

As with other motivational systems, the power motive is assumed to be stimulated by incentives whose attainment is associated with positive affective consequences. For the power motive, the incentive is the experience of influence, which in turn is associated with positive experiential qualities such as a sense of strength (cf. McClelland 1985). Interindividual differences in the power motive come from different experiences of positive (reward) and negative (punishment) consequences of acting with power in early childhood. For example, McClelland and Pilon (1983) surveyed mothers' parenting techniques and predicted the motives of now adults from the parameters thus obtained over 25 years later. The predictor of a high power motive turned out to be the tolerance that mothers showed their 5-year-old children toward aggressive behavior. The authors interpreted this correlation in such a way that the less strict control and sanctioning of behaviour enabled the experience of influence and the affective consequences associated with it.

In the book "Power – The inner experience" McClelland (1975) discusses right at the beginning that there are many different actions which at first glance do not have much in common and which would at best correlate moderately with each other when tested empirically. However, they all induce a similar feeling of strength and power "Different actions, same effect: a feeling of power"(McClelland 1975). It can be concluded that the feeling of strength as the actual motivational goal can be achieved through very different behaviors. McClelland's concern was to classify these expressions of power action. The two dimensions of classification are the source of power, which can be either within or outside the person, and the object of power, which can be either the self or the other. McClelland, borrowing from Erikson's stages of ego development, views the resulting four types of power as developmental stages that a person passes through from childhood to adulthood. The stages build on each other, but not every person reaches the highest stage.

#### ▪ Different Stages of Power

In power stage I, the leaning power striving (source: others, object: self), the source of power is outside the person (e.g., reading power-oriented magazines), but strengthens the self by at least allowing it to feel strong and powerful. The stage is also paraphrased as "it strengthens me." It originates in early infancy, where the mother or other caregivers have provided the milk and emotional support necessary for survival. Here the source of power comes from outside or another person and strengthens the self. Later in life, this form of power continues to express itself in drawing strength from others, such as one's partner or a leader.

Power stage II, also called self-related power striving (source: self, object: self), is characterized, for example, by the collection of prestige goods such as expensive cars or influential positions, with which the individual also strengthens the self, but this time through his own actions. In the spirit of "I strengthen myself," the child learns to control his or her own bodily functions during cleanliness education. In adulthood, this power modality manifests itself in a self-centered striving for power that aims to "control" other things, such as expensive cars and money, that represent a part of one's identity. Individuals at this stage also tend to have strong self-control and self-discipline.



In power stage III, the source of power is in the person but relates to others who are to be defeated, such as in competitive sports. After the child has learned to control himself, he learns that he can succeed in controlling others and an awareness of "I have influence over others" can form. Beginning with physical assertion of one's own interests and aggression, this power modality evolves in adulthood to more subtle forms of influence, such as persuading others, helping others, and negotiating skillfully and strategically. While power-motivated individuals at this stage find pleasure in showing others their powerlessness, they are also charming and good judges of character with great empathy.

One form of expression of power stage IV. (source: others, object: others) is to join influential organisations such as political parties or religious associations or even powerful corporations and to act in their interests, as it were as an instrument of this source of power, and to influence others. This reflects an external source of power with other individuals as objects of power. Individuals at this stage are credited with setting aside self-interest in favor of the interests of the organizations they serve, possessing high self-control, and demonstrating social skills. They can argue persuasively and win others to their cause.

#### ▪ Implications for Thinking

Like the achievement motive and the connection motive, the power motive influences perception and thinking. In the following, we explain how the power motive determines responsiveness to power stimuli, affective response to power stimuli, recall of power-themed content, and learning. The power motive makes individuals particularly responsive to power stimuli. As is true for the other implicit motives, the power motive sensitizes individuals to perceive motivationally relevant information and elicits stronger responses to it. This is because the power motive acts like an affect amplifier (cf. Schultheiss 2008). It makes the attainment of power-themed incentives more rewarding for high power motivators than for low power motivators.

Accordingly, high power motivators report higher perceived activation in response to power-themed talk (cf. Steele 1977) and when playing computer games with power incentives (cf. Schultheiss and Brunstein 1999). The excitation of the power motive and the power-themed stimuli associated with it may well occur unconsciously. The power motive also determines the affective response to power incentives. One affective response that is relatively independent of conscious influence is facial expression, which is objectively measurable, for example, by the electromyographic activity of facial muscles. Fodor and others took advantage of this (2006). They had high and low power motivators watch a video of either a person who presented as very determined and assertive (power stimulus group) or a person who presented as moderate to submissive (control group). They found the stronger affective response of high power motivators confirmed: These frowned more intensely when confronted with another person's dominance than low-power motivators and than high-power motivators in the control group.

The power motive also influences information intake and memory performance. As expected, this only applies to information relevant to the power motive. Highly power-motivated individuals remember the contents of their own biography, their everyday life, or the contents of fictional stories better than lowly power-motivated individuals if the contents are power-themed but not otherwise (cf. McClelland 1984; Woike 1995; McAdams et al. 1996). The power motive has been acquired through early learning experiences, but it also influences learning the other way around when power-themed information is in play. Following the principle of classical conditioning, for example, stimuli (abstract entities) that occur simultaneously with power stimuli (faces expressing dominance) elicit similarly strong responses (avoidance of attentional focus on dominant faces) as the original power stimuli.

Following the principle of operant conditioning, for example, behaviors that lead to power-themed success (such as superiority over others, low dominance of the counterpart) are learned better than behaviors that bring about power-themed failure (such as defeat, high dominance of another person). Recent experimental work testing the relationship between power motive and learning found evidence that conscious learning processes are not necessarily responsible for power-motivated behavior (see Schultheiss and Rohde 2002). Based on the principle of operant conditioning, Schultheiss et al. (2005) hypothesize and find empirical confirmation that individuals with a strong power motive showed improved learning performance in a task staged as a competition (visuomotor reaction task) when they previously emerged as winners (= power-related reward). After a defeat (= power-related punishment), impairments in a subsequent learning session were shown in accordance with the hypothesis.

**Background Information**

Expressions of the power motive

The power motive is associated with a variety of behavioral correlates, including holding office, preferring competitive sports, writing letters to the editor or online comments, owning prestige goods, consuming alcohol, and consuming sports and erotic content (cf. Winter 1973). Recent studies of the power motive show that its expressions are far more subtle than heavy-handed physical aggression against others or the display of prestige goods (cf. Schultheiss and Brunstein 1999). Thus, high power motivators were judged to be more competent and persuasive, with the means of influence being gestures and facial expressions (for example, raising the eyebrows to emphasize the importance of what was being said) rather than verbal arguments. At work, high power motivators excel in strategically planned careers that often result in leadership positions. In addition, power-motivated individuals prefer professions in which influence can be exerted, such as in teaching, where influence is exerted on the development of students' knowledge; as a pastor, who teaches religious norms; and as a psychotherapist, who supports individuals in weaker positions. But also in private life there are numerous opportunities for influence in all directions. Power-motivated people set the mood at parties, own many luxury goods and impress others with high-risk gambling behaviour.

As described above, the power motive can manifest itself in a wide range of behaviors. The commonality - the desired feeling of strength - has already been addressed. A striking difference in power-motivated behavior is whether it is directly aimed at influencing others or whether it consists of obtaining a sense of strength through surrogate actions without direct confrontation with others. Although early methods of power motive measurement already suggested that the power motive is expressed in a fear component "fear of losing power" or also called fear of losing control and a hope component "hope for power", also called hope for control, it was not until the multi-motive grid (cf. Sokolowksi and Schmalt 1996) that it was possible to capture a hope and fear component separately. With this distinction, the diversity of power actions can be ordered: "Fear of losing power"-motivated individuals prefer substitute gratifications such as consuming sports and sex content and consuming alcohol, which entail a sense of superiority, but at the same time eliminate the risk of losing power by avoiding actual interaction partners. "Hope for power" motivators, on the other hand, seek actual influence over others. Their confidence in succeeding in power situations allows them to confront others. For example, they assume important positions and offices and lead, direct, and guide others quite explicitly as leaders.



At first glance, one might think that individuals in management positions are characterized by a desire to perform uniquely and to single-mindedly seek opportunities for optimization and development. However, if one thinks more specifically about concrete tasks that managers have to perform, McClelland's finding that the achievement motive plays a rather minor role in large firms is not surprising (1975). Managers must above all be able to instruct and motivate others, precisely to direct and lead. This is a field of activity that suits power-motivated people. Performance-motivated people are hindered by their factual orientation, which manifests itself in a frequently not always very economical optimisation of details and an orientation towards the task itself rather than the people involved. As early as 1975, McClelland suspected that the constellation of motives of a successful manager was a combination of a high power motive with a high inhibition tendency and at the same time a low connection motive. McClelland called this constellation the "motive leadership pattern" (1975). These individuals exercise "socialized power"in the sense of responsible leadership of employees in the service of corporate goals (power stage IV.). They are characterized by loyalty, enthusiasm, and structured leadership that is valued by employees. In a classic study testing these relationships, McClelland and Boyatzis found their assumptions confirmed (1982). They measured motives of employees of the then large and powerful American Telephone and Telegraph Company and observed career developments over several years. As predicted, the "leadership motive pattern"measured at the beginning of the career correlated with the attainment of senior management positions after 8 and 16 years. However, the assumption of the described leadership motive pattern (high power, high inhibition, low connection) was not supported in all studies. Also, a high expression of all three components, i.e. also of the connection motive, was related to leadership effectiveness (cf. Steinmann et al. 2015). Among other things, the desire for power is already evident in career choice. Abele et al. showed that university graduates with a high power motive particularly often aspired to professions with high prestige and sphere of influence (cf. Abele et al. 1999).

**Background Information**
Company sizes and power motives

The advantages of a high power motive seem to be limited to certain company sizes and structures. Thus, the power motive unfolds its positive effect primarily in large companies with a strong hierarchical structure. In smaller companies with flat hierarchies, on the other hand, individual performance is more important than leadership performance. Here, high-performance motivated individuals are also frequently found successfully in leadership positions. A high performance motive also seems to be more significant than a strong power motive for the start-up of a company. For example, Wainer and Rubin were able to predict the economic success (measured by business turnover) of newly founded companies from the combination of a high achievement and low connection motive (1971).

Although it is true in principle that a high power motive is associated with holding management positions and successful career development (cf. McClelland and Franz 1992), there are also disadvantages of a high power motive. For example, Fodor and Farrow revealed as weaknesses of high power motivators that they could be influenced by flattery of their co-workers in the evaluation of job performance (cf. Fodor and Farrow 1979). In fictitious power situations, they also tended to contribute less factual information to group discussions and to disregard the views of their employees when making decisions.

## Literature

Abele, A. E.; Andrä, M. S.; Schute, T.: Wer hat nach dem Hochschulexamen eine Stelle? Erste Ergebnisse einer Längsschnittstudie. Zeitschrift für Arbeits- und Organisationspsychologie, 43/1999, S.95–101

Ainsworth, M. D.; Blehar, M. C.; Waters, E.; Wall, S. N.: Patterns of attachment: A psychological study of the strange situation, New York 1978

Andrews, J. O. W.: The achievement motive and advancement in two types of organization. Journal of Personality and Social Psychology, 6/1967, S.163–168, S.164

Atkinson, J. W.: Motivational determinants of risk-taking behavior. Psychological Review, 64, 359–372. 1957, S. 360; S.362

Atkinson, J. W.: Motives in fantasy, action, and society. Princeton 1958, S. 361

Bandura, A.: Self-efficacy: Toward a unifying theory of behavioral change. Psychological Review, 84/1977, S.191–215

Baumeister, R., & Leary, M. R.: The need to belong: Desire for interpersonal attachments as a fundamental human motivation. Psychological Bulletin, 117/1995, S.497–529

Bischof-Köhler, D.: Zur Phylogenese menschlicher Motivation. In: L. H. Eckensberger; E.-D. Lantermann (Hrsg.): Emotion und Reflexivität, S. 3–47, München 1985

Bowlby, J.: The nature of the child's tie to his mother. Interactional Journal of Psychoanalysis, 39/1958, S.350–373

Deci, E. L.; Ryan, R. M.: Intrinsic motivation and self-determination in human behaviour, New York 1985

Deci, E. L.; Ryan, R. M.: The »what« and »why« of goal pursuits: Human needs and the self-determination of behavior. Psychological Inquiry, 11/2000, S.227–268.

DeWall, C. N.; MacDonald, G.; Webster, G. D.; Masten, C.; Baumeister, R. F.; Powell, C. : Acetaminophen reduces social pain: Behavioral and neural evidence. Psychological Science, 21/2010, S.931–937

Dickhäuser, O.: Fähigkeitsselbstkonzepte: Entstehung, Auswirkung, Förderung. Zeitschrift für Pädagogische Psychologie, 20/2006, S.5–8

Eisenberger, N. I.; Liebermann, M. D.; Williams, K. D.: Does rejection hurt? An fMRI study of social exclusion. Science, 302/2003, S.290–292

Fodor, E. M.; Farrow, D. L.: The power motive as an influence on use of power. Journal of Personality and Social Psychology, 37/1979, S.2091–2097

Fodor, E. M.; Wick, D. P.; Harsen, K. M.: The power motive and affective response to assertiveness. Journal of Research in Personality, 40/2006, S.598–610

French, E. G.: Development of a measure of complex motivation. In: Atkinson, J.W. (Ed.): Motives in fantasy, action, and society, Princeton 1958a, S.242–248

French, E. G.: Effects of the interaction of motivation and feedback on task performance. In: Atkinson, J.W. (Ed.): Motives in fantasy, action, and society, S.400–408, Princeton 1958b

French, J. R. P.; Raven, B. H.: The basis of social power. In: Carwright, D.(Ed.): Studies in social power (pp. 150–167). Ann Arbor 1959

Gable, S. L.: Approach and avoidance social motives and goals. Journal of Personality, 74(1)/2006, S. 175–222

Heckhausen, J.; Heckhausen, H.: Motivation und Handeln, Berlin 2018;

Heckhausen, H., Schmalt, H.-D., & Schneider, K.: Achievement motivation in perspective. New York, NY: Academic 1985

Heider, F.: The psychology of interpersonal behavior. New York 1958

Isaacson, R. L.: Relation between achievement, test anxiety and curricular choices. Journal of Abnormal and Social Psychology, 68/1964, S.447–452.

Kelley, H. H.: Attribution theory in social psychology. In D. Levine (Ed.), Nebraska symposium on motivation. Lincoln 1967

Lewin, K.: Field theory in social sciences, Chicago 1951

Litwin, G. H.; Siebrecht, A.: Integrators and entrepreneurs; their motivation and effect on management. Hospital Progress, 48(9)/1967, S.67–71

Mahone, C. H.: Fear of failure and unrealistic vocational aspiration. Journal of Abnormal and Social Psychology, 60/1960, S.253–261

McAdams, D. P.; Hoffmann, B. J.; Mansfield, E. D.; Day, R.: Themes of agency and communion in significant autobiographical scenes. Journal of Personality, 65/1996, S.339–377

McClelland, D. C.: Power: The inner experience, New York 1975, S.12

McClelland, D. C.: The empire-building motivational syndrome, in: McClelland, D.C. (Ed.): Motives, personality, and society: Selected papers (pp. 147–174) New York 1984

McClelland, D. C.: Human motivation, Glenview 1985

McClelland, D. C.; Boyatzis, R. E.: Leadership motive pattern and long-term success in management. Journal of Applied Psychology, 67/1982, S.737–743

McClelland, D. C., & Franz, C. E.: Motivational and other sources of work accomplishment in mid-life: A longitudinal study. Journal of Personality, 60/1992, S.679–707

McClelland, D. C.; Pilon, D. A.: Sources of adult motives in patterns of parent behavior in early childhood. Journal of Personality and Social Psychology, 44/1983, S. 564–574

McClelland, D. C.; Atkinson, J. W.; Clark, R. A.; Lowell, E. L.: The achievement motive. New York 1953

McClelland, D. C.; Koestner, R., Weinberger, J.: How do self-attributed and implicit motives differ? In C. P. Smith, J. W. Atkinson, D. C. McClelland, & J. Veroff (Eds.), Motivation and personality: Handbook of thematic content analysis 1992 (pp. 49–72). (Originally published as an article in "Psychological Review," 1989, 96, 690–702) Cambridge University Press

McKeachie, W. J.: Motivation, teaching methods, and college learning. In: Jones. M.R. (Ed.), Nebraska Symposium on Motivation 1961 (pp. 111–142), Lincoln 1961

Mehrabian, A.; Ksionsky, S.: A theory of affiliation. Lexington 1974

Meyer, W.-U.: Das Konzept von der eigenen Begabung. Bern 1984

Murray, H. A.: Exploration in personality. New York 1938, S.82

Schultheiss, O. C.: Implicit motives. In O. P. John, R. W. Robins & L. A. Pervin (Eds.), Handbook of personality: Theory and research (3rd ed., pp. 603–633), New York 2008, p.264

Schultheiss, O. C.; Brunstein, J. C.: Goal imagery: Bridging the gap between implicit motives and explicit goals, Journal of Personality, 67/1999, S.1–38

Schultheiss, O. C.; Rohde, W.: Implicit power motivation predicts men's testosterone changes and implicit learning in a contest situation. Hormones and Behavior, 41/2002, S.195–202.

Schultheiss, O. C.; Wirth, M. M.; Torges, C.M.; Pang, J.S.; Villacorta, M. A.; Welsh, K. M.: Effects of implicit power motivation on men's and women's implicit learning and testosterone changes after social victory or defeat. Journal of Personality and Social Psychology, 88(1)/2005, S.174–188

Schuster, B.; Försterling, F.; Weiner, B.: Perceiving the causes of success and failure. A cross-cultural examination of attributional concepts. Journal of Cross-Cultural Psychology, 20/1989, S.191–213.

Sokolowksi, K.; Schmalt, H.-D.: Emotionale und motivationale Einflussfaktoren in einer anschlusst-hematischen Konfliktsituation. Zeitschrift für Experimentelle Psychologie, 18/1996, S.461–482

Sorrentino, R. M.; Sheppard, B. H.: Effects of affiliation-related motives on swimmers in individual versus group competition: A field experiment. Journal of Personality and Social Psychology, 36/1978, S.704–714

Steele, R. S.: The physiological concomitants of psychogenic motive arousal in college males. Unpublished dissertation thesis, Boston 1977

Steinmann, B.; Dörr, S. L.; Schultheiss, O. C.; Maier, G. W.: Implicit motives and leadership performance revisited: What constitutes the leadership motive pattern? Motivation and Emotion 39(2)/2015, S.167–174

Stiensmeier-Pelster, J.: Erlernte Hilflosigkeit, Handlungskontrolle und Leistung. Göttingen 1988

Stiensmeier-Pelster, J., Schürmann, M., Eckert, C., & Pelster, A.: Attributionsstil- Fragebogen für Kinder und Jugendliche (ASF-KJ). Göttingen 1994

Wainer, H. A.; Rubin, I. M.: Motivation of research and development entrepreneurs: Determinants of company success. In: Kolb, D.A.; Rubin, I.M.; McIntire, J. (Eds.), Organizational Psychology (pp. 131–139). Englewood Cliffs 1971

Weiner, B.: A theory of motivation for some classroom experiences. Journal of Educational Psychology, 71/1979, S.3–25

Weiner, B.; Frieze, I. H.; Kukla, A.; Reed, L.; Rest, S.; Rosenbaum, R. M.: Perceiving the causes of success and failure. New York 1971

Winter, D. G.: The power motive. New York 1973

Woike, B. A.: Most-memorable experiences: Evidence for a link between implicit and explicit motives and social cognitive processes in everyday life. Journal of Personality and Social Psychology, 68/1995, S. 1081–1091.

# Self-Determination Theory

Contents




A. Moring, *AI on The Job*,
https://doi.org/10.1007/978-3-662-64005-0_6

With intelligent and autonomous systems in companies, the question of who determines and makes or is allowed to make decisions inevitably arises for the people who (should) work with these systems. This is about the self-determination of humans, which can be restricted in various areas by AI-based technologies, because these technologies take over decision domains from humans. This in turn has repercussions on motivation and identification with the company and one's own job. The self-determination theory claims to explain these interrelationships.

## 6.1 Self-Determination and Motivation



Self-determination theory (SDT), as a macro theory of human motivation, addresses such fundamental issues as personality development, self-regulation, universal psychological needs, life goals and aspirations, energy and vitality, unconscious processes, as well as the relationship between (corporate) culture and motivation, and the effects of social environments on people's motivation, affect, behavior, and well-being. The theory thus relates to issues within a wide range of life domains. In the context of this study, particular focus will be placed on aspects of the relationship between organizational culture and motivation, as well as the effects of social environments on motivation. Although the earliest work leading to the development of SDT dates back to the 1970s and the first relatively comprehensive explanation of the theory appeared in the mid-1980s (Deci and Ryan 1985), research has developed particularly strongly since the turn of the millennium. Fundamental research extending and refining motivational principles has continued at an energetic pace since then, with the largest quantitative increase in published SDT studies most notable in the fields of sport, education and healthcare. In contrast, there is a gap in research and validation of the SDT model here in relation to work environments dominated by technology.

**Background Information**

Differentiation of the types of motivation

Many historical and contemporary theories of motivation treated the phenomenon of motivation primarily as a unified concept. These theories looked at the overall scope, so to speak, of people's motivation in particular behaviors or activities. Self-determination theory began with the differentiation of types of motivation. The original idea is that the type or quality of a person's motivation was more important than the overall level of motivation. This should allow better predictions to be made, for example, about mental health and well-being, a person's effective performance, creative problem solving, and deep or conceptual learning.

Self-determination theory as a whole provides a broad framework for the study of human motivation and personality. SDT (◘ Fig. 6.1) articulates a meta-theory for the framework of motivational studies, a formal theory that defines intrinsic and various extrinsic sources of motivation, and a description of the respective types of intrinsic and types of extrinsic motivation in human cognitive and social development and in individual differences (cf. Deci and Ryan 1985, 2000; Ryan and Deci 2017). Perhaps more importantly, SDT proposals also focus on how social and

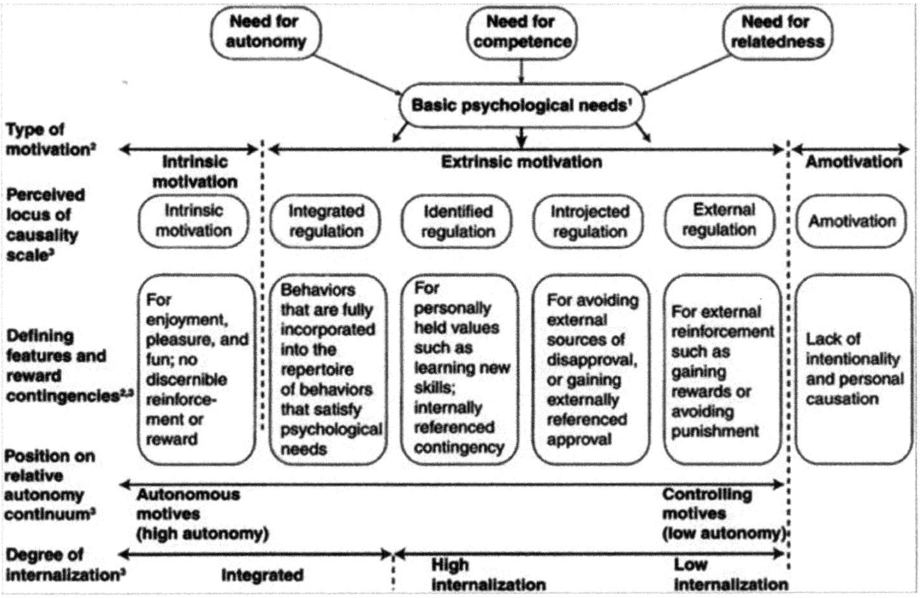


**Fig. 6.1** Model of the self-determination theory

cultural factors promote or undermine people's spirit of will and initiative, in addition to their well-being and the quality of their performance. It is argued that conditions that support the individual experience of autonomy, competence, and being included foster the most volitional and highest quality forms of motivation and engagement in activities, including improved performance, persistence, and creativity. Moreover, SDT asserts that the degree to which any of the three psychological needs of autonomy, relatedness, and competence are not supported or even prevented in a social context will have a robust, detrimental impact on well-being in that setting.

The dynamics of psychological need support and need satisfaction have been examined within families, classrooms, teams, organizations, clinics, and cultures using specific criteria considered authoritative within SDT. The SDT model thus has both broad and behavioral implications for understanding practices and structures that enhance or diminish need satisfaction and a person's resulting full performance. These implications range from basic research on motivational micro-processes to applied clinical studies, the results of which are in principle transferable to other social and professional domains.

Self-determination theory is thus a so-called organismic-dialectical approach. It begins with the assumption that humans are active organisms, with distinct strivings for growth, for coping with challenges of their own environment, and for integrating new experiences into a coherent self-concept or self-awareness. However, these natural developmental tendencies do not operate automatically; instead, they require ongoing social conditions and support for this striving. That is, the social context can either support or counteract the natural tendencies toward active engagement and psychological development. In that case, a lack of (social) integration, security, and personal fulfillment can lead people to seek out a so-called need substitute, which will be discussed later. Thus, this is the dialectic between the active organism and the social context that forms the basis for SDT's predictions about human behavior, experience, and development.

## 6.2 Connection with the Basic Principles of Connection, Performance, Power



Within SDT, the basic requirements for healthy development and performance are specified using the previously described concept of basic psychological needs for autonomy (power), competence (achievement), and relatedness (connection). To the extent that these needs are met on an ongoing basis, people will develop and perform effectively and experience a sense of well-being of their own. If these needs are not met on an ongoing basis or over an extended period of time, people are more likely to become ill and experience a sharp decline in their ability and willingness to perform. The "dark sides" of human behaviour and experience, such as certain types of psychopathology, prejudice and aggression, are to be understood as reactions to the non-fulfilment of basic needs, because the environment does not permit this due to its circumstances or because fulfilment is deliberately denied.

### ▪ Six Connected Theories

Formally, SDT comprises six sub-theories (cf. Curran 1980; Deci and Ryan 1985; Houston 1986), each of which was developed to explain a range of motivational phenomena that have been identified in laboratory and field research. Each of these theories, therefore, addresses a facet of motivation or personality performance.

1. Cognitive evaluation theory (CET) refers to intrinsic motivation, a motivation based on the satisfaction of behaving "for its own sake". Prototypes of intrinsic motivation are children's exploration or play. Intrinsic motivation is thereby a lifelong creative source. Research specifically addresses the effects of social contexts on intrinsic motivation or how factors such as rewards, interpersonal controls, and personality interactions influence intrinsic motivation and interest in things. The research highlights the crucial role that the factors of competence and autonomy play in fostering intrinsic motivation, which is critical in education, the arts, sports, and, of course, work.
2. The second sub-theory, Organismic integration theory (OIT), addresses the topic of extrinsic motivation in its various forms, with its characteristics, determinants, and effects. Broadly speaking, extrinsic motivation is behavior that is instrumentally characterized and aimed at outcomes manifesting in the individual's external world. In addition, there are various forms of instrumentality that include external regulation, introjection, identification, and integration.

These subtypes of extrinsic motivation are to be understood along a continuum of internalization of the individual's experiences. The more extrinsic motivation is internalized, the more autonomous the individual will be in engaging in his or her typical behaviors. OIT is further concerned with social contexts that promote or inhibit internalization. Here, it examines what causes people to resist, partially adopt, or even deeply internalize values, goals, or belief systems. In particular, OIT highlights support for autonomy and relatedness as crucial criteria for internalization.

3. Causality orientations theory (COT) describes individual differences in people's tendencies to orient to the environment and regulate their behavior in different ways. COT describes and evaluates three types of causality orientations: autonomy orientation, in which individuals act out of interest in and appreciation of events and their environment; control orientation, which focuses on rewards, gains, and approval or affirmation; and impersonal or motivated orientation, which is characterized by competence anxiety.
4. Basic psychological needs theory (BPNT) describes the concept of developed psychological needs and their relationship to psychological health and well-being. BPNT argues that psychological well-being and optimal performance and motivation are based on autonomy, competence, and relatedness. Therefore, contexts and environments that support or counteract these needs should invariably affect a person's well-being. The theory argues that all three needs are essential and that when any of these needs are denied or hindered, significant losses in performance and motivation result. Because basic needs are universal aspects of performance, the BPNT is concerned with cross-developmental and cross-cultural settings to validate and refine the model.
5. Goal contents theory (GCT), relies on the distinction between intrinsic and extrinsic goals and their effects on motivation and well-being. Goals are considered to be objectives if they differentially enable the satisfaction of basic needs and therefore can be differentially associated with well-being. Extrinsic goals such as financial success, appearance, and popularity/fame were specifically contrasted with intrinsic goals such as community, close relationships, and personal growth, with the former more likely to be associated with lower well-being and greater unhappiness, and vice versa.
6. Attachment, which has to do with establishing and maintaining close personal relationships such as with best friends or one's life partner, as well as belonging to groups, is one of the three basic psychological needs, as described earlier. The sixth sub-theory, relationships motivation theory (RMT), addresses these and other relationships of people in their personal environment and assumes that some level of such interactions is not only desirable for most people, but even essential for their social integration and interaction, as well as for their well-being, since the relationships satisfy the need for connectedness and affiliation. However, research shows that in high-quality relationships, not only is the need for connectedness satisfied, but also the need for autonomy and, to a lesser extent, the need for competence. Indeed, the highest quality personal relationships are those in which each partner supports the autonomy, competence, and relatedness needs of the other.

As SDT has evolved, both theoretical considerations and empirical findings have led to the investigation of a variety of processes and phenomena relevant to personality growth, effective performance, and well-being. For example, SDT research has focused on the importance of "mindfulness" as a basis for autonomous regulation of behavior, which has led to both refined methods of measurement and further theorizing about human consciousness. Research on conditions conducive to intrinsic motivation led to more detailed explanations and measurement methods related to vitality, as an indicator of both mental and physical well-being. The work on vitality also uncovered, among other things, the positive influence of experiences of nature on well-being – a connection that should arouse particular interest against the background of an increasingly mechanised and autonomous world of work and everyday life. Some work within SDT research has explored in more detail the forms that personal passions can take, with individuals developing obsessively or harmoniously depending on internalization processes. Cross-cultural tests of SDT have led to a better understanding of how economic and cultural forms affect the unchanging aspects of human nature. The study of well-being has also led to new theories and research on the valuation of well-being itself, including the distinction between hedonic and eudaimonic forms of life. Specific research themes such as autonomy versus controlled motivation have led to a better understanding of internalized control such as ego-involvement and contingent self-esteem, as well as a deeper understanding of the differences between these aforementioned categories and autonomous self-regulation.



**Background Information**

Fields of application of the SDT

In addition to formal theory development, SDT research has been applied in many areas, including career and work, education, organizational development, sport, religion, health and medicine, parenting, virtual environments and media, relationships, and psychotherapy. In these areas, research has examined how controlling versus autonomy-enhancing environments affect performance and well-being, as well as achievement and persistence. In addition, the positive impact of connectedness and competence is seen to correlate with volitional support in promoting engagement and esteem within specific settings and activity domains. This body of applied research has now led to considerable specification of techniques, including goal structures and modes of communication, that have been shown to be effective in promoting sustained volitional motivation.

### ▪ Autonomous or Controlled Motivation?

The most central distinction in SDT is thus that between autonomous motivation and controlled motivation. Autonomous motivation includes both intrinsic motivation and the types of extrinsic motivation in which people have identified with the value of an activity and ideally have even integrated it into their self-concept. When people are autonomously motivated, they actively experience their willpower or experience self-affirmation through their actions. Controlled motivation, in contrast, consists of both external regulation, where one's behavior is a function of external contingency factors of reward or punishment, and internal regulation, when the regulation of action has been partially internalized and is determined by factors such as the approval motive, avoidance of shame, conditional self-esteem, and self-involvement. When people are externally or internally controlled, they experience pressure to think, feel, or behave in certain ways. Autonomous and controlled motivation can lead to energetic and direct behavior. Previous research, has confirmed across domains that autonomous motivation and controlled motivation lead to very different outcomes. Autonomous motivation tends to lead to greater psychological health and more effective performance in people across very different types of activities. Autonomous motivation also leads to long-term persistence, for example, when it comes to maintaining change toward healthier behaviors. Research on autonomous and controlled motivation has also extended to studies of unconscious processes. Studies using so-called priming methods and implicit appraisal have shown how the motivational processes and principles of SDT operate, at both conscious and unconscious levels. The advantages of autonomous motivation have been confirmed at all levels (cf. Levesque et al. 2008).

Deci and Ryan, in their research on intrinsic motivation and internalization, were able to present and prove the hypothesis that there are a number of universal psychological needs that must be satisfied in order to work effectively and that are conducive to mental health. Further research in a variety of countries-including cultures with collectivist, traditional values and others with individualistic, egalitarian values-has confirmed that the satisfaction of the needs for competence, autonomy, and relatedness (connection) can indeed predict the psychological well-being of people in all cultures and societies; SDT thus relies in large part on the three dimensions of motivation connection, achievement, power, described in detail earlier. Although some "cultural relativists" claimed that, for example, the need for autonomy is only important in cultures that value individualism and less important in cultures that value collectivism, this turned out not to be the case. Feelings of autonomy, such as competence and relatedness, are essential to a healthy and capable state of the individual in a wide range of highly diverse cultures. The concept of human needs proves extremely useful because it provides a means of understanding how different social forces and interpersonal environments influence autonomous and controlled motivation. Here, it lends itself to examining whether a particular contextual factor, such as a monetary reward, an opportunity for choice, or a performance evaluation, makes it more likely that, in humans, the effects of that factor on motivation, behavior, an affect, and well-being can be predicted. The same is true, of course, when the aforementioned contextual factors are not present and whether negative effects can then be predicted. The basic needs postulate described above helps to explain why only some effective behaviors actually increase well-being, while others do not.

**Background Information**

Need satisfaction level

Many motivational theories have as their primary goal to distinguish in the individual the strength of one or more psychological needs; for example, for the need for achievement, for intimacy, or for control. The idea is that needs are learned, and some people develop stronger needs than others. Self-determination theory now claims that the needs for competence, relatedness and autonomy are basic and universal. The individual distinctions within the theory do not focus on differences in the strength of the needs, but instead focus on how the degree of satisfaction of the needs affects motivation and psychological well-being. Specifically, there are two general individual difference concepts within SDT: causality orientations and life goals.

Causality orientations are general motivational orientations that refer to: (a) the ways in which people orient themselves in relation to the environment and how these attitudes relate to the initiation and regulation of behavior, and (b) the extent to which they are generally self-determined in various domains and situations. Three orientations exist in this regard: autonomous, controlled, and impersonal. The development of a strong autonomy attitude results from sustained satisfaction of all three basic needs. The development of a strong controlled attitude results from some satisfaction of the competence and relatedness needs and from a failure to satisfy the autonomy need. The development of an impersonal attitude results from a general failure to satisfy all three needs. According to SDT, people have some level of each of the three attitudes. One or more of these attitudes can be used to make predictions about various psychological or behavioral effects. There is a consistent positive relationship between the autonomy attitude to psychological health and to effective, i.e., productive and high-performing, behaviors. The controlled attitude leads to rigid ways of functioning and working and decreased well-being. The impersonal attitude leads to dysfunction and symptoms of illness, such as self-loathing and lack of vitality.



#### ▪ Long-Term Goals

Other empirical work within SDT research relates to the long-term goals that guide people in their activities. Empirically, these goals fall into two general categories, referred to as intrinsic aspirations and extrinsic aspirations. Intrinsic aspirations include life goals such as belonging, generativity, and personal development. Extrinsic aspirations include goals such as wealth, fame, and attractiveness. Numerous studies have shown that a focus on intrinsic goals, relative to extrinsic goals, is associated with greater health, well-being, and performance (see Vansteenkiste et al. 2004). Aspirations have been studied in terms of their strength or importance and, as such, have similarities to what are termed needs and motives in other fields of research. In SDT, however, these aspirations are explicitly not considered needs, because needs here are essential necessities rather than learned desires. Instead, aspirations are understood as functions that describe the degree to which basic needs for competence, relatedness, and autonomy are satisfied or denied over a period of time. For example, when needs have been thwarted, people tend to adopt extrinsic goals based on external indicators of value rather than the internal feelings that result from the satisfaction of needs. As such, extrinsic pursuits are a type of need substitution: they provide little or no direct satisfaction, but people pursue these goals because they hope to substitute or compensate for the lack of genuine need satisfaction. In pursuing extrinsic goals, people tend to suppress the pursuit of basic need satisfaction.

#### ▪ Developments and Extensions

In recent years there have been many developments and extensions of the SDT model, only two of which will be briefly described here. Self-determination theory has always postulated that the development of integrated, autonomous behaviors depends on the person's awareness. Studies of mindfulness define this concept as an open awareness and interested attention to what is happening within and around oneself (cf. Brown and Ryan 2003). This mindfulness has been associated with autonomous motivation and a variety of positive psychological and behavioral effects. Accordingly, the promotion of mindfulness or awareness has been theorized as a key element of psychotherapy that allows for inner exploration, reflective inquiry into people's needs and feelings, and promotes the development of a more autonomous orientation.

Another important aspect of motivation concerns the energization of people's psychological processes and behaviors. According to SDT, the energy for action comes either directly or indirectly from basic psychological needs. The concept of vitality in the SDT model here refers to the energy that is available to the individual, that is, the energy that is intoxicating and the resulting empowerment that enables people to act more autonomously and focus more and longer on the important activities. While other theories have postulated that self-regulation and choice promote energy, SDT research has hypothesized and demonstrated that only controlled regulation consumes energy (see Moller et al. 2006). Autonomous regulation is not exhaustive for the individual, but can instead be vitalizing. Self-determination theory likewise reasons that controlled motives drain energy from the individual and that actions directed at satisfying needs can actually affect the energy available for self-regulation.

## Literature

Brown, K. W.; Ryan, R. M.: The benefits of being present: Mindfulness and its role in psychological well-being. Journal of Personality and Social Psychology, 84/2003, S. 822–848

Curran, Bernard: A Critique of Deci's "Cognitive Evaluation Theory", Loretto 1980

Deci, E. L.; Ryan, R. M.: Intrinsic motivation and self-determination in human behaviour, New York 1985

Deci, E. L.; Ryan, R. M.: The "what" and "why" of goal pursuits: Human needs and the self-determination of behavior. Psychological Inquiry, 11/2000, S. 227–268.

Houston, Ronald: A Comprehensive Analysis of Cognitive Evaluation Theory: Effects of Performance Contingent Reward and Positive Feedback on Intrinsic Motivation, Idaho 1986

Levesque, C.; Copeland, K. J.; Sutcliffe, R. A.: Conscious and nonconscious processes: Implications for self-determination theory. Canadian Psychology, 49/2008, S. 218–224

Moller, A. C.; Deci, E. L.; Ryan, R. M.: Choice and egodepletion: The moderating role of autonomy. Personality and Social Psychology Bulletin, 32/2006, S. 1024–1036

Ryan, R. M.; Deci, E. L.: Self-determination theory: Basic psychological needs in motivation, development, and wellness, The Guilford Press 2017.

Vansteenkiste, M.; Simons, J.; Lens, W.; Sheldon, K. M.; Deci, E. L.: Motivating learning, performance, and persistence: The synergistic effects of intrinsic goal contents and autonomy-supportive contexts. Journal of Personality and Social Psychology, 87/2004, S. 246–260

# Jobs Demands Resources

Contents




A. Moring, *AI on The Job*,
https://doi.org/10.1007/978-3-662-64005-0_7

Motivation and productivity do not depend solely on personal psychological circumstances and interdependencies at the individual level of the person. Circumstances and the endowment of resources is also an important factor. We can only do things well and achieve goals if we have the means to do so. These means can be tangible and intangible. Since companies work and manage with people and resources, this insight is particularly significant. The JD-R model represents the described connections and interdependencies. It is therefore very well suited to answer the question of what people in companies need in order to work productively and motivated with AI-based systems and technologies and to achieve their goals and those of their company.

## 7.1 Basic Assumptions



The job demands-resources model (JD-R) (cf. Demerouti et al. 2001; Bakker et al. 2003a) is based on the assumption that each occupation has its own specific risk factors associated with stress at work (◘ Fig. 7.1). These factors can be classified into two general categories: These categories are the (specific) work demands and the work resources in an occupation or job. This defines an overarching model which can be applied to different occupational situations and which is initially independent of the specific requirements and resources associated with the particular "job" in terms of content. Job demands here refer to the physical, psychological, social or organisational aspects of work. They are sustained physical as well as

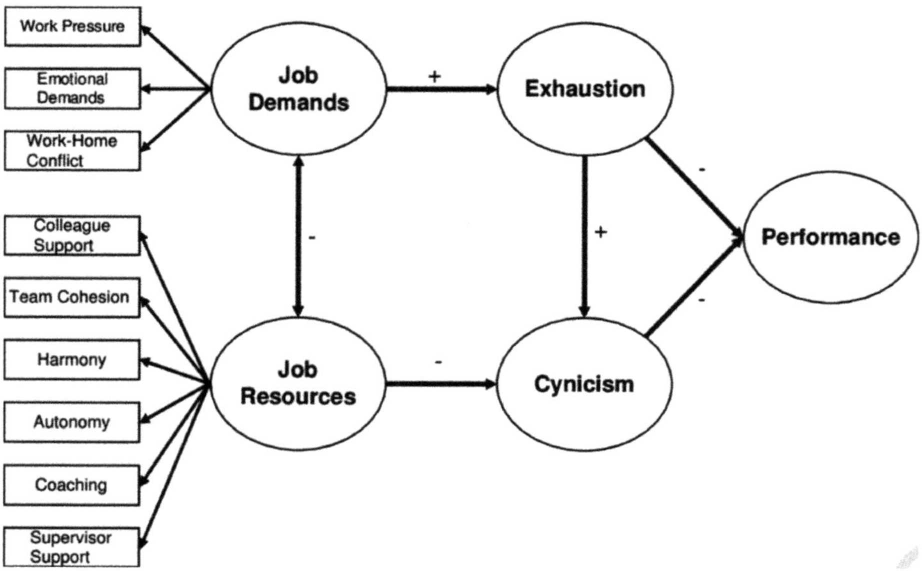


◘ **Fig. 7.1** The Jobs demands-resources model

psychological (cognitive and emotional) efforts or skills necessary for the job and applied in the job, which are therefore associated with certain physiological and/or psychological costs. Examples of these "costs" include high work pressure, an unfavorable physical environment, or emotionally demanding interactions with customers. Although work demands are not necessarily negative per se, they can turn into so-called stressors at work. This is the case when the fulfilment of these demands requires a high level of effort from which the employees then cannot sufficiently recover (cf. Meijman and Mulder 1998).

**Definition**

Labour resources

The work resources considered in the model refer, as already mentioned, to physical, psychological, social or organisational aspects of a job or activity, which can be characterised as follows:

- They fulfil an important function in the achievement of work objectives
- They lead to a reduction in work demands and the associated physiological and psychological costs.
- They stimulate personal growth, learning and personal development.

Therefore, resources are not only necessary to meet work requirements, but are in themselves fundamentally important for the fulfilment of "jobs" in both a quantitative and qualitative sense. This connection is also described in a work by Hackman and Oldham already from 1980. In the so-called "characteristics theory", the motivational potential of work resources is related to the task level, including autonomy, feedback and task importance (cf. Hackman and Oldham 1980). Furthermore, at a more general level, the conservation of resources theory (COR) describes that primary human motivation is due to the conservation and accumulation of resources (cf. Hobfoll 2002). Accordingly, resources are valued by people because of their independent nature or because they are means to achieve or protect other valuable resources. Resources may be located in different places and at different levels throughout the organisation. They may relate, for example, to salary, or to (potential) career, opportunities, job security, and just as they may relate to interpersonal and social relationships on the job, for example, the relationship with the supervisor, the perceived quality of employee support, or the team climate. Resources can also relate to the organisation of work, for example, clarity of roles, participation in decision-making in one's own area, and also to the level of the task to be performed, for example, the variety of skills required and demanded in the job, the quantity and quality of the tasks to be performed, perceived importance of the task, autonomy in performing the task, or receiving or not receiving performance feedback (it is precisely these resources that are addressed in the questions in the survey described later in the following chapter of this study).

## 7.2 Duplicate Processes

A second basic assumption of the JD-R model is that two different underlying psychological processes play a role when it comes to the interaction of workload and motivation. First basic assumption: Work-related health impairment, poorly designed workplaces or chronically high work demands (e.g. work overload, emotional demands) deplete employees' mental and physical resources. This can therefore lead to the depletion of employees' energy and motivation and, by extension, to more serious health problems (see Leiter 1993; Demerouti et al. 2001). Individuals, on the other hand, in turn use strategies to protect performance depending on the environmental demands at hand. Such performance protection can be achieved by, on the one hand, a so-called mobilization of sympathetic activation (autonomic and endocrine activation) and/or, on the other hand, by increased subjective effort (defined as the use of active control in information processing). Thus, the greater the activation and/or effort, the greater the physiological costs to the individual. These physiological costs due to increased activation and/or subjective effort are referred to as "compensation costs". As a result of these costs or efforts, strategy adjustments can occur in the form of a narrowing of attention, increased selectivity or a redefinition of the task requirements. Fatigue may also set in, in the form of riskier choices and decisions and a high degree of subjective fatigue. The long-term effect of such a compensatory strategy manifests itself in a decrease in an individual's energy, which can eventually lead to a complete breakdown.



The second basic assumption presented by the JD-R model is motivational in nature. Here, it is assumed that work resources have motivational potential and lead to high engagement at work, as well as lower cynicism in dealing with employees and excellent performance. This leads to the following definition: work resources can either play an intrinsic motivational role because they promote and encourage employee growth, learning and development or they play an extrinsic motivational role because they are critical to the achievement of work goals. In the first case, work resources fulfill basic human needs (cf. Deci and Ryan 1985), such as the needs for autonomy (cf. DeCharms 1968), competence (cf. White 1959), and relatedness (cf. Baumeister and Leary 1995). For example, appropriate feedback promotes learning, which increases job competence, while appropriate decision latitude and social support satisfy the need for autonomy and the need for relatedness, respectively. Work resources can just as clearly play an extrinsic motivational role, because according to the effort recovery model (cf. Meijman and Mulder 1998), resources in the respective work environments promote employees' willingness to devote their own efforts and skills to the work task. In this case, it is likely that the task will be successfully accomplished and that the work goal will be achieved. For example, supportive colleagues and proper feedback from the supervisor can increase the likelihood of being successful in achieving one's work goals. In both cases, whether through the satisfaction of basic needs or the achievement of work goals, the presence of work resources leads to engagement, while their absence results in a cynical attitude toward work. This study's own quantitative survey and its analysis in the following chapters are intended to shed light on which resources are most relevant to intrinsic and/or extrinsic motivation.

## 7.3 Interactions Between Work Demands and Resources

In addition to the main effects of work demands and resources just described, the JD-R model posits that the interaction between work demands and work resources is important for the development and perception of workload and motivation. Specifically, it presents that work resources can buffer the effects of job demands on workload, including burnout (see Bakker et al. 2003b). This claim is quite consistent with Karasek's (1998) job demand control model (DCM); the JDR model now extends this DCM model by postulating that several different work resources could play the role of a buffer for several different work demands. Where exactly demands and resources play a role in a particular organization depends on the specific job characteristics that are prevalent in each case. Thus, while the DCM model indicates that control over task performance (autonomy) can buffer the effects of work overload on job stress, the JD-R model extends this view and states that in different types of jobs, job resources may interact in predicting job stress.

This claim is consistent with Diener and Fujita's (1995) findings that many potential resources may facilitate the achievement of a particular goal or requirement, implying that different goals or requirements are likely to be influenced by multiple resources. This so-called buffer hypothesis is also consistent with Kahn and Byosserie (1992), who argue that the buffer or interaction effect described is between each pair of variables in a kind of tension-strain relationship. They posit that characteristics of the work situation, as well as the characteristics of the individual, can equally buffer the effects of a stressor. This buffering variable can reduce the impact of the characteristics of the work organization on the individual, it can modify specific stressors, it can influence perceptions and cognitions, it can have a moderating effect on reactions and assessment situations, or it can mitigate health-damaging consequences of high demands (cf. Kahn and Byosserie 1992). Social support, i.e. help from colleagues and superiors, is probably the best known of these situational variables, which appears as a potential buffer against occupational stress (cf. Johnson and Hall 1988).

**Definition**

Moderators and "buffers"

Other criteria in work situations that can act as moderators or "buffers" are:

- The extent to which the onset of a stressor is predictable (e.g., role clarity and performance feedback).
- To what extent the reasons for the presence of a stressor are comprehensible (e.g. through information from superiors or institutions).
- The extent to which aspects of the stressor can be controlled by the individual and whether that individual can experience it (e.g., work autonomy).

The reason why such work resources outlined above can act as buffers is different for different resources. For example, a quality relationship with one's supervisor can buffer and mitigate the impact of job demands (e.g., work overload, emotional and physical demands) on perceived job stress because the leader's appreciation and support put job demands in a different perspective. Leaders who actively and credibly provide appreciation and support can also help the employee cope with high or new job demands, facilitate performance and even protect against work-related illness in the medium and long term. Comparatively, work autonomy may also be crucial for employee health and well-being because greater autonomy in employee perceptions and appraisals is associated with more opportunities to cope with stressful situations (cf. Jenkins 1991). Social support in this sense is a straightforward resource, as it is very good at assisting in the achievement of work goals. It is precisely this importance of social support and especially backing from superiors that is particularly evident in the quantitative findings of this study in the results later. Thus, support from colleagues can help to get the job done on time, and this can mitigate the effects of possible work overload (cf. Van der Doef and Maes 1999). Moreover, the stress buffering hypothesis described here states that social support protects workers from pathological consequences of stressful experiences (cf. Cohen and Wills 1985).



Another example: Constructive feedback not only helps employees do their jobs more effectively, it also improves communication between supervisors and employees. When specific and accurate information is provided in a constructive way, it leads to both employees and supervisors being able to improve their performance or adapt and change to new challenges (see also the expectation for technical training and transparency in the workings of AI systems as a prerequisite for employee cooperation with these new systems, as described in the following chapters). Appreciating employees for good performance helps to maintain their motivation and signals them to continue in this direction (cf. Hackman and Oldham 1980). In addition, communicating with employees in a positive way when they need to improve their performance and it helps to avoid possible future work problems.

#### ▪ High Work Demands

Another fundamental aspect of the JD-R model is that work resources have a particular effect on motivation or work engagement when work demands are high. According to the "theory of conservation of resources" (COR), people try to preserve, maintain and protect what they value, for example various material, social, personal or energetic resources (cf. Hobfoll 2001).

**Background Information**

Stress and loss of resources

The JD-R model posits that stress experienced by individuals should be understood in relation to the potential or actual loss of resources. Hobfoll and Shirom have justified these relationships as follows (2000):

- The individual must bring in resources to prevent the loss of resources.
- Individuals with a larger pool of resources are less vulnerable to resource loss.

- Those individuals who do not have access to strong resource pools are the ones who are likely to suffer further and increasing losses (known as the "loss spiral").
- Strong resource pools lead to a greater likelihood that individuals will seize opportunities to risk their own resources for even greater resource gains (so-called "winning spiral").

Hobfoll has additionally argued that a resource gain in itself has only a modest effect and acquires its real significance in the context of the (actual or potential) loss of resources. This implies that work resources develop their motivational potential especially when workers are confronted with high work demands. The introduction of new systems and technologies without prior experience in the organisation or on an individual level, such as AI systems, may well be understood and categorised as such a high work demand.

## 7.4 Evidence for the JD-R Model

Several studies have now provided clear evidence for the hypotheses put forward by the JD-R model. Specifically, a number of studies support the concept of a so-called dual pathway to good and productive collaboration hypothesized by the model; they also showed important organizational connections. In 2003 (cf. Bakker et al. 2003a), Bakker et al. applied the JD-R model to call center employees of a Dutch telecommunications company and investigated its predictive validity for employees' self-reported absenteeism and expectations of actual turnover achieved in that area. Results from a series of analyses based on structural equation modeling (SEM) broadly support the dual process relationships. With respect to energy-driven processes, it was job demands, such as work pressure, computer problems, emotional demands, and changes in tasks, that were the most important predictors of health problems. In relation to sickness absence, in relation to permanent and long-term absence there was also evidence. In relation to motivation-driven processes associated with work resources, for example, social support or supervisory coaching, performance feedback and time control, it could be seen that these could serve as predictors of commitment and organisational engagement, even predicting expected turnover.

Hakanen et al. found comparable results among Finnish teachers in their study. Specifically, they found that high levels of work demands were related to poor health and even burnout, and that work resources affected job engagement and organizational commitment (Hakanen et al. 2006). In addition, Bakker et al. applied the JD-R model to food production employees and were able to use it to predict future registered absence from work (cf. Bakker et al. 2003a).The results of the SEM analyses, in turn, showed that job demands may be particularly good predictors of burnout and, indirectly, of duration of absence, while job resources may be very good predictors of organizational commitment and, indirectly, of duration of absence. Finally, Bakker et al. used the JD-R model to examine the relationship between job characteristics, burnout, and other performance ratings (see Schaufeli and Bakker 2004). They found that the most highly rated job demands (e.g., work pressure and emotional demands) in each case were also the most important predictors of exhaustion components of burnout and also predicted job performance. In contrast, job resources (e.g., autonomy and social support) were the most important predictors of additional role performance or, conversely, decreasing engagement. Taken together, these findings support the JD-R model's contention that job demands and job resources influence two distinct psychological processes, which in turn ultimately influence important organizational outcomes of processes and operations in organizations (cf. Bakker et al. 2003b; Schaufeli and Bakker 2004).

Most studies provide evidence for the dual process relationships proposed by the JD-R model based on subjective assessments of job demands and resources. Two additional studies used an alternative methodology for assessing job demands and resources. The study by Demerouti et al. among workers who work with people, systems, or information, observers received subjects' ratings of job demands and resources in addition to self-reports (2001). The results of a series of structural comparison analyses, using both self-report data and observer ratings of job characteristics, provide strong and consistent evidence for the validity of the JDR model. Job demands were primarily positively related to job exhaustion, whereas available work resources were primarily negatively related to demotivation and absence from work.



A 2005 study by Bakker et al. looked at employees from seven different organizations who were asked to use the Utrecht Work Engagement Scale (the UWES). In the first step, 20 employees with high engagement and 20 employees with low engagement were visited at their workplace and confronted with short video clips of about 30 s. The video clips were played by professionals. In these video clips, professional actors acted out two aspects of possible work engagement (vigor and dedication) in relation to three work demands and four work resources. Participants were asked to indicate how often they had experienced each of the situations shown on the video clips. The results showed that the engaged group more often reported their own experiences that matched the work engagement (drive and dedication) portrayed in the role play in the video. Importantly here, the low-commitment group and the high-commitment group also differed significantly in terms of the frequency of several work conditions shown in the video clips. Specifically, as predicted, job resources (not job demands) were higher for the high engagement subjects. The high engagement group scored significantly higher on three of the four job resources present in their work environment. The resources here are autonomy, feedback, and supervisory coaching; the effect of social support was rather insignificant in the case. There were no differences between the two groups in terms of work demands here.

## 7.5 Evidence of the Buffering Effect of Labour Resources

Two studies explicitly address the buffer effect of work resources on the interaction between work demands and well-being just outlined and find clear evidence for the described relationship. In their study of 1000 employees at a large university, Bakker et al. find that the combination of high demands and low work resources contributes significantly to the prediction of burnout; exhaustion and cynicism are used here as markers and criteria (Demerouti and Euwema 2003). Specifically, they found that work overload, emotional demands, physical demands, and accessibility at work and at home did not lead to high levels of burnout when employees experienced autonomy in their work environment, received feedback, had social support, or maintained high-quality relationships with their supervisors. Psychologically, different processes and effects may have been responsible for these interaction effects. Perceived autonomy may have helped in coping with job demands because employees could decide for themselves when and how to respond to demands in their jobs. Experienced social support and a quality relationship with the supervisor may have cushioned the impact of work stresses because employees received instrumental help and emotional support. Furthermore, feedback may have been helpful because it gave employees information that was helpful or necessary for maintaining their performance and staying healthy (see Kahn and Byosserie 1992).

Similar results were obtained by Xanthopoulou et al. who tested the jobs-demands-resources interaction hypothesis (2007). Perceived autonomy was found to be the most important buffer against burnout in the face of high job demands, followed by support from others and perceived opportunities for personal career development. The results of the study showed that all significant interactions were consistent with the JD-R interaction hypothesis. In situations where job demands were high and job resources were low at the same time, this led to maximum exhaustion and cynicism. Conversely, in situations where the level of job resources was high, the effects of high job demands on the level of exhaustion were significantly reduced.

An older study outside the framework of the JD-R model addresses the hypothesis that resources become more important in the context of high demands or even threats. Billings et al. found that men who cared for AIDS patients while experiencing social support maintained their positive emotional states. They also had fewer detectable physical symptoms of distress under stressful conditions, underscoring the importance of resource gain in the context of potential resource loss (as described earlier) (see Billings et al. 2009). Two studies using the JD-R model also showed that job resources in particular have an effect on work engagement, especially when job demands are high. Hakanen et al. tested this interaction hypothesis on a sample of Finnish dentists in the public sector (2006). It was hypothesized that job resources (e.g., variability in required job skills or peer contacts) would be most beneficial for maintaining job engagement under conditions of high job demands (e.g., workload, unfavorable physical environment). Dentists were divided into two random groups for the purpose of cross-validating the results. A series of hierarchical regression analyses yielded 17 of 40 significant interactions (40%), showing, for example, that variability in job skills increased work engagement when qualitative workload was high and moderated the negative effects of qualitative workload on work engagement.

Conceptually similar findings were developed by Hakanen et al. (2007). n their study of Finnish teachers working in primary, secondary, and vocational schools, they found that work resources act as buffers and that there were negative relationships between student misbehavior and work engagement. In addition, they found that work resources particularly influenced work engagement when teachers were faced with high levels of student misbehavior. A series of moderated structural equation models revealed 14 of 18 possible two-way interaction effects (78%). In particular, supervisor support, innovativeness, esteem, and organizational climate were important work resources for teachers that helped them deal with challenging situations with students and students.



## 7.6 Conclusion on the Job Demands-Resources Model

While the JDR model fits into the tradition of the general demand-control model (cf. Karasek Jr. 1979) effort-reward-imbalance model, it also meets the requirement for specificity by examining different types of job demands and resources, depending on the occupational context (cf. Demerouti et al. 2001). Thus, the JDR model encompasses and extends both models and is much more flexible and rigorous. Van Veldhoven et al. validated the model with data from 37,291 Dutch workers (2005). They found that the model was able to represent the best approximation of the relationships between work characteristics, health and well-being. Similarly, Lewig and Dollard's study of Australian call centre workers showed that the JD-R model allowed for higher variance in emotional exhaustion and job satisfaction than either the DCM or ERI models (2003).

> Four main areas for future research on the JD-R model can currently be defined in principle. These relate to the reciprocal relationships, the objective outcomes, the main and interaction effects and the inclusion of personal resources in the JD-R model.

The classical hypotheses that job demands and job resources can predict workload and motivation in a conventional way have been confirmed by several studies (cf. Wong et al. 1998; De Jonge et al. 2001; Dormann and Zapf 2002). However, is it also conceivable that employee well-being affects job demands and job resources? In their review, Zapf et al. (1996) identified an inverse causal relationship between work conditions and demonstrated job stress in 6 of 16 longitudinal studies. More recent studies provide additional evidence of reverse causality, for example, between the financial prospects of the self-employed and their health (see Gorgievski-Duijvesteijn et al. 2000, 2005), between the quality of the doctor-patient relationship and burnout (see Bakker et al. 2000), as well as between job characteristics (e.g., job control, job complexity, supervisor support, work pressure, and lack of separation between job and personal life) and exhaustion or satisfaction (cf. Wong et al. 1998; Demerouti et al. 2004; De Lange et al. 2004). Two studies elaborated evidence for reverse causal effects over a time lag of five (cf. Bakker et al. 2000) and even 10 years (cf. Gorgievski-Duijvesteijn et al. 2000). In addition, Houkes (2002) examined several job resources in bank employees and teachers in a long-term research and also found evidence of a reverse causal effect between a motivational potential environment (including variety of skills, task identity, task importance, autonomy, and job feedback) and intrinsic work motivation. Finally, Salanova et al. (2006) found that organizational resources were good predictors of work-related flow in the future.

Taken together, these findings suggest that job stress and motivation are both outcomes and predictors of job demands and resources, such that higher stress and less favorable working conditions negatively affect motivation over time. Thus, there are several possible explanations for such reverse causal effects. Two explanations have already been briefly discussed here. Employees who suffer from job stress will subsequently exhibit withdrawal behavior when faced with additional demands and fewer resources at the same time. For example, such employees who are exhausted by their work are likely to fall behind in their work processes, which means additional pressure life and may result in role conflict in the organization (see Demerouti et al. 2004). Similarly, employees may also engage in behaviors such that they "depersonalize" their customers and partners, so to speak, treating them as objects rather than human beings, because personal and empathic interactions are likely to be perceived as more demanding and stressful (cf. Bakker et al. 2000).

**Background Information**

The "loss spiral"

Such findings are consistent with the principle and image of a "loss spiral" (cf. Hobfoll 2001, 2002). Moreover, job requirements and resources in the respective work environment can also be influenced by employees' perceptions (cf. Zapf et al. 1996). Just as depressed people's tendency to view their environment more negatively leads to a negative climate (cf. Beck 1972), burned-out employees may perceive their job demands as relatively high and complain more frequently about their workload, thus creating a negative work climate (cf. Bakker et al. 2000). Similarly, engaged employees may use more resources and thus even be better able to mobilize their resources because they are perceived as more pleasant colleagues to work with. Indeed, social information processing theory argues that general attitudes toward one's work – such as cynicism toward work or, in the other case, dedication – emerge in a process in which individuals cognitively construct the characteristics of their work in relation to their social context (cf. James and Tetrick 1986; Wong et al. 1998).

Both explanations of reverse causal effects are also pertinent to the phenomenon of workers taking action to shape, form and redefine their jobs (cf. Wrzesniewski and Dutton 2001) The shaping of a job involves the shaping of the task boundaries of the job (either physical or cognitive) and the relationships with other task descriptions and jobs. Thus, people are not purely passive recipients of information from their work environment, but rather active in interpreting their work and consequently in designing their jobs (cf. Daniels 2006). Future studies on the JD-R model should aim to include reverse causal relationships as well and promote further insights into the phenomenon of job design and thus into the dynamics of employee well-being.

Most studies on the JD-R model have relied exclusively on self-report methods. Some exceptions to this rule include Demerouti et al. who used expert ratings to assess job demands and job resources, Bakker et al. and Salanova et al. who used other performance assessments, or who used video recordings to examine job demands and resources. It is crucial for further research to include in studies and models objective criteria and methods that play a role in business. For example, Harter et al. in their study of about 8000 business units in 36 companies showed that the level of employee engagement is positively related to the performance of the particular business unit, that is, it is dependent on, for example, customer satisfaction and loyalty, profitability, productivity, turnover, and the stability and security of the business. The authors conclude that employee engagement is "... associated with business outcomes achieved at a magnitude that is relevant and important for many organizations to evaluate" (Harter et al. 2002). Future research should further elucidate the extent to which objective economic indicators (e.g., job performance, customer satisfaction, illness, absenteeism, sales) can be predicted by the JD-R model. It would also be interesting to examine whether the presented combinations of job demands and resources can predict objective health outcomes or specific risks.



#### ■ Open Questions on the JD-R Model

Studies on the JD-R model as well as on the DCM indicate that there is indeed evidence and proof for the main (additive) effects of job demands and job resources on strain and motivation as well as for the described interaction effects, which, however, have not yet been sufficiently investigated. This is either because the researchers concerned have shown more interest in studying main effects or because interaction effects are simply more difficult to detect (cf. Van der Doef and Maes 1999). However, it seems worthwhile that future studies pay more attention to both perspectives because each perspective may have different theoretical and practical implications. On a theoretical level, it is important to work out what happens to perceived stress when work demands and work resources are raised to an increased level – quite a situation that is often encountered in several occupations in the course of digitalisation. Does this change also lead to a high level of perceived strain (cf. the additive main effects model), or to a low or medium level of strain (cf. interaction effects)? The answer to this question has very practical implications. If work resources do indeed cushion the impact of work demands on strain, then it is obvious that organizations will need to increase their work resources if they need to change the level of work (cf. Van Vegchel 2005). In a statistical sense, it is important to know whether the interaction follows a multiplicative function, which would mean that work resources determine the strength of the relationship between work demands and strain, or whether a proportional or ratio function is more appropriate to describe the relationships here (cf. Edwards and Cooper 1990). This latter assumption implies that strain increases as the proportion of job demands in the tasks to be performed increases and resources simultaneously (relatively) decrease (cf. Van Vegchel 2005). As Edwards and Cooper (1990) present, a preference for one or the other type of interaction should be based on theoretical foundations that have yet to be developed in research. An important extension of the JD-R model is the inclusion of personal resources in the model. Most recently, Xanthopoulou et al. examined the role of three personal resources, self-efficacy, organization-related self-esteem, and optimism, in predicting work exhaustion and absenteeism (see Xanthopoulou et al. 2007).

**Background Information**

Personal resources alone are not enough

The JD-R model assumes that each occupation has its own specific work characteristics, that these characteristics in turn can be divided into two general categories (precisely the work requirements and work resources). It thus represents an overarching model that can be applied to different occupational situations regardless of the specific requirements and resources. The central assumption of the JD-R model is that job strain increases – regardless of the nature of the job or occupation – when (certain) job demands are high and when (certain) job resources are limited. In contrast, motivated work engagement is most likely when work resources are high and even when work demands are very high. Various results of structural equation modeling analyses show that personal resources are not sufficient to balance the relationship between work demands and exhaustion. Meaning, therefore, that the company is under an obligation to contribute its own part to a "sufficient" resource endowment. However, it could be shown that personal resources partly influence the relationship between work resources and work engagement, which suggests that the resources available in the company or in the job simultaneously promote the development of personal resources.

This means that the JD-R model can be considered as a suitable tool for human resource management as a whole. As each job can have its own unique risk factors for exhaustion, demotivation and even burnout, a two-stage procedure was established in organisational research in connection with the JD-R model. The first qualitative stage of the research involves exploratory interviews with job holders from different levels of an organisation's hierarchy, e.g. senior management, middle management and shop floor staff. The interviews, which last about 45 min, include open-ended questions about the interviewees' jobs and are designed to shed light on the positive and negative aspects. This qualitative phase is valuable in research because it can potentially generate knowledge about unexpected, organization-specific job demands and job resources that would be overlooked in highly standardized approaches. For example, it is conceivable that in one organization (e.g., a manufacturing company) employees are exposed to high physical work demands, while in another organization (e.g., an insurance company) employees are not exposed to such demands at all. In addition, in certain organizations, employees face mergers or acquisitions, which invariably entail uncertainty about the future of one's jobs and role ambiguity. Such organization-specific job requirements are best elicited and considered in a qualitative exploratory phase. This two-phase approach has also been the model for this study on artificial intelligence in companies and employee motivation: Via exploratory interviews with experts and practitioners in the first phase and comprehensive interviews and surveys of (potentially) "affected" employees.

In the second phase of the survey, the work demands and potential work resources associated with exhaustion or engagement are operationalised in so-called items and scales and included in a tailor-made questionnaire. All employees in an organization are then invited to complete this questionnaire. This enables a quantitative analysis of the situation in the company. The aim here is to find out whether and how the qualitatively identified requirements and work resources potentially play a role in the perception of workload and motivation. The analysis usually focuses on differences between departments and workplaces, in terms of specific demands and resources, and in terms of employee well-being and potential

> **The Right Resources Determine Success**
> In summary, empirical evidence supports the notion that work resources are responsible for two distinct processes. Accordingly, work demands are related to perceived stress, manifested by a lack of energy and the development of health problems, and work resources are related to motivation, manifested by a commitment to or withdrawal from the work task, each in a clear relationship. This alone is certainly not too surprising... However, combining these relationships in an additive sense leads to the following deductions. When both job demands and resources are high, employees can be expected to develop their own motivation even when stressed, whereas when both factors are low, employees can be expected to exhibit strain and demotivation. Consequently, high demands and low resources imply a state of high strain and low motivation, while low demands and high resources result in a low sense of strain and high motivation. It should be borne in mind here that this can also lead to a feeling of being underchallenged in the long term, which can also have a negative effect on motivation in the medium and long term. It is therefore a question of the right balance or "levelling" of requirements and resources.



consequences. Further sub-group analysis can provide clear indications of appropriate interventions, as it highlights and highlights the strengths and weaknesses of departments and workplaces. Tailored interventions are then possible with the aim of reducing the identified work demands and providing the important work resources to reduce the risk of burnout and increase the likelihood of committed work engagement and good performance.

## Literature

Bakker, A.B.; Schaufeli, W.B.; Sixma, H.; Bosveld, W.; Van Dierendonck, D.: Patient demands, lack of reciprocity, and burnout: a five-year longitudinal study among general practitioners, Journal of Organizational Behavior, Vol. 21/2000, S.425–41

Bakker, A.B.; Demerouti, E.; De Boer, E.; Schaufeli, W.B.: Job demands and job resources as predictors of absence duration and frequency. Journal of Vocational Behavior, 62/2003a, S.341–356

Bakker, A.B.; Demerouti, E.; Schaufeli, W.B.: Dual processes at work in a call centre: An application of the Job Demands – Resources model. European Journal of Work and Organizational Psychology, 12/2003b, S.393–417

Baumeister, R., & Leary, M. R.: The need to belong: Desire for interpersonal attachments as a fundamental human motivation. Psychological Bulletin, 117/1995, S.497–529

Beck, A.T.: Depression: Causes and Treatment, Philadelphia 1972

Billings, D.W.; Folkman, S.; Acree, M.; Moskowitz, J.T.: Coping and physical health during caregiving: the roles of positive and negative affect, Journal of Personality and Social Psychology, Vol. 79/2009, S.131–42

Cohen, S. and Wills, T.A.: Stress, social support, and the buffering hypothesis, Psychological Bulletin, Vol. 98/1985, S.310–50

Daniels, K.: Rethinking job characteristics in work stress research, Human Relations, Vol. 59/2006, S.267–90

De Jonge, J.; Dormann, C.; Janssen, P.P.M.; Dollard, M.F.; Landeweerd, J.A.; Nijhuis, F.J.N.: Testing reciprocal relationships between job characteristics and psychological well being: a cross-lagged structural equation model, Journal of Occupational and Organizational Psychology, Vol. 74/2001, S.29–46

De Lange, A.; Taris, T.W.; Kompier, M.; Houtman, I.; Bongers, P.: The relationships between work characteristics and mental health: examining normal, reversed and reciprocal relationships in a four-wave study, Work and Stress, Vol. 18/2004, S.149–66

DeCharms, R.: Personal causation. New Jersey 1968

Deci, E. L.; Ryan, R. M.: Intrinsic motivation and self-determination in human behaviour, New York 1985

Demerouti, E., Euwema, M.: Job Resources Buffer the Impact of Job Demands on Burnout. Journal of occupational health psychology. 10/2003 S.170–180

Demerouti, E.; Bakker, A.B.; Nachreiner, F.; Schaufeli, W.B.: The job demands resources model of burnout. Journal of Applied Psychology, 86/2001, S.499–512

Demerouti, E.; Bakker, A.B.; Bulters, A.J.: The loss spiral of work pressure, work-home interference and exhaustion: reciprocal relations in a three-wave study, Journal of Vocational Behavior, Vol. 64/2004, S.131–49

Diener, E.; Fujita, F.: Resources, personal strivings, and subjective well being: a nomothetic and idiographic approach, Journal of Personality and Social Psychology, Vol. 68/1995, S.926-35

Dormann, C.; Zapf, D.: Social stressors at work, irritation, and depressive symptoms: accounting for unmeasured third variables in a multi-wave study, Journal of Occupational and Organizational Psychology, Vol. 75/2002, S.33–58

Edwards, J.R.; Cooper, C.L.: The person-environment fit approach to stress: recurring problems and some suggested solutions, Journal of Organizational Behavior, Vol. 11/1990, S.293–307

Gorgievski-Duijvesteijn, M.J.; Giessen, C.; Bakker, A.B.: Financial problems and health complaints among farm couples: results of a ten-year follow-up study, Journal of Occupational Health Psychology, Vol. 5/2000, S.359-73

Gorgievski-Duijvesteijn, M.J.; Bakker, A.B.; Schaufeli, W.B.; Van der Heijden, P.G.M.: Finances and health: a dynamic equilibrium model of resources, Journal of Occupational Health Psychology, Vol. 10/2005, S.210–24

Hackman, J. R.; Oldham, G.R.: Work redesign. Reading 1980

Hakanen, J.J.; Bakker, A.B.; Schaufeli, W.B.: Burnout and work engagement among teachers, Journal of School Psychology, Vol. 43/2006, S.495–513

Hakanen, J., Demerouti, E., Xanthopoulou, D.: Job Resources Boost Work Engagement, Particularly When Job Demands Are High. Journal of Educational Psychology. 99/2007.

Harter, J.K.; Schmidt, F.L.; Hayes, T.L.: Business-unit-level relationship between employee satisfaction, employee engagement, and business outcomes: a meta-analysis, Journal of Applied Psychology, Vol. 87/2002, S.268–79

Hobfoll, S.E.: The influence of culture, community, and the nested-self in the stress process: Advancing conservation of resources theory. Applied Psychology: An International Review, 50/2001, S.337–370

Hobfoll, S.E.: Social and psychological resources and adaptation, Review of General Psychology, Vol. 6/2002, S.307–24

Hobfoll, S.E.; Shirom, A.: Conservation of resources theory: Applications to stress and management in the workplace, in: Golembiewski, R.T. (Ed.): Handbook of Organization Behavior, Dekker, New York 2000, S.57–81

Houkes, I.: Work and individual determinants of intrinsic work motivation, emotional exhaustion and turnover intention, Maastricht 2002

James, L.R.; Tetrick, L.E.: Confirmatory analytic tests of three causal models relating job perceptions to job satisfaction, Journal of Applied Psychology, Vol. 71/1986, S.77–83

Jenkins, R.: Demographic aspects of stress, in: Cooper, C.L., Payne, R. (Eds.): Personality and Stress: Individual Differences in the Stress Process, Wiley, New York 1991, S.107–32

Johnson, J.V.; Hall, E.M.: Job strain, work place social support and cardiovascular disease: a cross-sectional study of a random sample of the Swedish working population, American Journal of Public Health, Vol. 78/1988, S.1336–1342

Kahn, R.L.; Byosserie, P.: Stress in organizations, in: Dunette, M.D.; Hough, L.M. (Eds): Handbook of Industrial and Organizational Psychology, Vol. 3, Consulting Psychologists Press, Palo Alto 1992 S.571–650

Karasek, R.A.: Demand/Control Model: A social, emotional, and physiological approach to stress risk and active behaviour development. In: Stellman, J.M. (Ed.): Encyclopaedia of occupational health and safety (pp. 34.6–34.14). Geneva 1998

Karasek Jr., R.A.: Job Demands, Job Decision Latitude, and Mental Strain: Implications for Job Redesign. In: Administrative Science Quarterly. Vol. 24, No. 2, June, 1979, S.285–308

Leiter, M.P.: Burnout as a developmental process: Consideration of models, in: Schaufeli, W.B.; Maslach, C.; Marek, T. (Eds.): Professional burnout: Recent developments in theory and research (pp. 237–250), Washington 1993

Lewig, K.A.; Dollard, M.F.: Emotional dissonance, emotional exhaustion and job satisfaction in call centre workers, European Journal of Work and Organizational Psychology, Vol. 12/2003, S.366–92

Meijman, T.F.; Mulder, G.: Psychological aspects of workload, in: Drenth, P.J.; Thierry, H.; de Wolff, C.J. (Eds.): Handbook of Work and Organisational Psychology (2nd ed.; pp. 5–33), Hove 1998

Salanova, M.; Bakker, A.B.; Llorens, S.: Flow at work: evidence for an upward spiral of personal and organizational resources, Journal of Happiness Studies, Vol. 7/2006, S.1–22

Schaufeli, W.B.; Bakker, A.B.: Job demands, job resources, and their relationship with burnout and engagement: a multi-sample study, Journal of Organizational Behavior, Vol. 25/2004, S.293–315

Van der Doef, M.; Maes, S.: The Job Demand-Control(-Support) Model and psychological well being: a review of 20 years of empirical research, Work and Stress, Vol. 13/1999, S.87-114

Van Vegchel, N.: Two models at work: a study of interactions and specificity in relation to the demand-control model and the effort-reward imbalance model, Utrecht 2005

Van Veldhoven, M.J.P.M.; Taris, T.W.; De Jonge, J.; Broersen, S.: The relationship between work characteristics and employee health and well being: how much complexity do we really need?, International Journal of Stress Management, Vol. 12/2005, S.3–28

White, R.: Motivation reconsidered: The concept of competence. Psychological Review, 66/1959, S.297–333

Wong, C.S.; Hui, C.; Law, K.S.: A longitudinal study of the job perception-job satisfaction relationship: a test of the three alternative specifications, Journal of Occupational and Organizational Psychology, Vol. 71/1998, S.127–46

Wrzesniewski, A.; Dutton, J.E.: Crafting a job: revisioning employees as active crafters of their work, Academy of Management Review, Vol. 26/2001, S.179–201

Xanthopoulou, D.; Bakker, A.B.; Demerouti, E.; Schaufeli, W; Taris, T.; Schreurs, P.: Different combinations of job demands and resources predict burnout, International Journal of Stress Management, Vol. 14/2007, No. 2, S.121–141

Zapf, D.; Dormann, C.; Frese, M.: Longitudinal studies in organizational stress research: a review of the literature with reference to methodological issues, Journal of Occupational Health Psychology, Vol. 1/1996, S.145–69

# Artificial Intelligence and Employee Motivation

Contents




A. Moring, *AI on The Job*,
https://doi.org/10.1007/978-3-662-64005-0_8

What do the changes in companies and jobs look like in concrete terms? What tasks will artificial intelligence take on and what tasks will humans take on? Answers to these and related questions can best be provided by those who already have experience in the development and application of artificial intelligence. From their knowledge and assessments, a qualified and at the same time empirically robust picture of future developments can be derived, which brings us one step closer to successful AI implementation in companies.

## 8.1 Requirements, Activities and Tasks in Cooperation with Artificial Intelligence



For the further investigation of the research question, the author chose the two-stage procedure method just described. However, it was not related to and applied in one company, but rather with different experts from different companies and industries for the qualitative and explorative interviews and with a free survey for the quantitative survey among participants from different companies and industries and at different levels of experience and career. This broad distribution naturally also means a certain degree of fuzziness in the statements and thus also in the following analyses and evaluations. However, considering the fact that this is the first survey regarding artificial intelligence in one's own work environment using the JD-R model, these weaknesses can be considered rather minor. In fact, the wide dispersion is capable of yielding a generally more valid picture and results, as it incorporates many different perspectives and sets of experiences in relation to the epistemic questions. In further research and for practical implementation in companies, the selection of respondents would of course have to be narrowed down and defined more precisely.

The use of systems and tools based on artificial intelligence will change the requirements for employees. These changes are complex. For example, the changes involve new job profiles, i.e. adapted descriptions of activities and responsibilities for certain positions in companies. But the changes are also about the elimination of activities and tasks because they can be processed faster, more efficiently and more reliably in automated and partly autonomous processes. This leads to these tasks and activities falling out of job descriptions, so to speak. This can lead to entire jobs being eliminated for employees because they are largely taken over by AI technologies and the "remaining" components of the (former) jobs are distributed to or merged with others. So again, this distribution and recomposition also represents another dimension of change. In addition, there will be further jobs and job descriptions with specific requirements that will arise in the first place through the use of AI systems and applications in companies.

All of this must inevitably result in further changes elsewhere in companies and organizations. Changes in the division of tasks and cooperation between humans and artificial intelligence also mean, for example, changes in process flows, hierarchies and decision-making powers. Decision-making authority within an organization can be transferred from one position to another or from humans to technology or a system. The same applies to the responsibilities for the functioning of processes. Here, too, the question must be asked whether it makes sense to continue to have people monitor, control and manage certain processes or whether this responsibility can be transferred to machines. These changes inevitably call existing hierarchies into question, because hierarchies are defined by monitoring and control rights and decision-making powers, as well as the associated responsibilities. Where and how these changes manifest themselves depends on the company and its own business. Therefore, these company-specific details will not be discussed further in this study. However, this is a worthwhile field for further research and analysis.

**Background Information**

Profiles for AI jobs

On a higher or more abstract level – i.e. a market level above the dimension of an individual company – the developments and changes mentioned can, however, be predicted and described. Subsequently, this also applies to new and changed requirements in activities that are characterized or even explicitly defined by collaboration with AI technologies. This results in describable profiles that show which experiences, which competencies, which characteristics and which knowledge are or will be required in such activities and jobs.

### ■ Interviews with Experts from Science and Practice

To this end, and with this insight objective in mind, several qualitative and exploratory interviews were conducted with experts who have in-depth knowledge and extensive experience in both the technical dimension and the dimension of business and human resource management. The interviews were conducted during 2019. The experts will be briefly described below.

The CEO of an internationally operating IT and service provider specializing in the development and implementation of solutions based on new communication channels and digital media (Interview 1). With a network of highly specialized companies, the company works for European industry leaders in the development of business models based on the new paradigms such as Big Data, Cloud Computing, Digital Media and the Internet of Things. Services offered include: Consulting, Systems Integration and Digital Services. A focus in development and implementation is on Artificial Intelligence. The company has been operating successfully in the market for several decades and can therefore rely on extensive expertise and experience in the areas of AI development and implementation and digital transformation.

The board of a likewise internationally active agency group (Interview 2). The company “produces talking points that move people”, according to its self-description. The company started out as a public relations agency and has now grown into a group of nine content agencies and specialist units offering all the disciplines of a content marketing agency and content creation. The company now has around 700 employees in the core disciplines of public relations, film and digital marketing at ten locations. Data science methods and AI technologies and applications are used in a wide range of areas. In addition, the agency group was one of the first companies in the industry to establish its own data science and AI team several years ago. This results in know-how and knowledge about the use of AI technologies for various goals and the adaptation of AI technologies to different customer requirements.

The managing director of a system and software provider for AI-based financial services (Interview 3). The company develops and markets AI-based solutions from the inventory and analysis of existing processes and data availability, to the development of a concrete digitalization roadmap, to the implementation of individually tailored solutions for the tax departments of companies from various industries and of different sizes. The portfolio includes consulting, implementation of AI technologies and tax apps, as well as accompanying training. This is intended to accelerate and optimize tax processes, realize savings, and ensure tax compliance. The company has experience and expertise in the development of its own AI technologies, as well as in the implementation and realization of these systems and tools in organizations.

The managing director of a Europe-wide service provider for performance marketing (Interview 4). The beginnings of performance marketing and thus also of the company's business lie in classic retargeting, i.e. the recognition and "tracking" of potential customers or Internet users who belong to a defined target group. Today's performance marketing has developed through the constant evolution of this approach into more specific criteria. For the current form of performance marketing, a huge amount of direct data and indirect data on specific conditions is available from a wide variety of sources. These huge inventories have to be checked and calculated over and over again for each customer and target by autonomous machines and systems in order to reach the optimum or at least come close to it. The company is thus able to define and predict states and characteristics for advertising optimization from the collected data; a technology and know-how that is also made available to other companies as a service. Thus, the company has a long experience in the use of AI technologies, their adaptation to a wide variety of goals and customer needs and the implementation of AI applications in their own company.



The managing director of a German commercial bank (Interview 5). The company is active in the business areas of private banking, investment banking, pension provision and the classic lending business with corporate and private customers. For this purpose, own products and services as well as those of cooperation partners are marketed. The bank was an early adopter of digital solutions and systems and continues to be an early adopter of technology. As a result, the company was and is very familiar with technology-driven innovations and changes, has many years of experience and can also provide valid assessments of future developments based on this.

The founder and CEO of a medical start-up (Interview 6). The company specializes in the market for medical image analysis. This field is growing significantly, but the number of cancer experts among medical professionals remains largely the same, resulting in a growing workload per specialist. The company develops and markets automation tools for visual diagnosis using artificial intelligence and so-called deep learning. The tools help cancer experts make reliable and reproducible diagnoses. This frees specialists from tedious, repetitive tasks such as quantifying cells or biomarkers, and should allow them to focus on tasks where their human expertise is indispensable. To this end, the company collaborates with leading pathology institutes and university laboratories. The company thus also has extensive experience and expertise both on the technical side and in implementation in highly specialized professional environments.

An internationally active consultant for organizational development and digital transformation (Interview 7). After several positions in international companies and corporations with personnel and business responsibility, this interview expert switched to consulting. For several years, large companies as well as medium-sized businesses have been among the clients who are confronted with the digital transformation of their business and their organization and who also want to implement new technologies and systems in the course of this. In the first cases, this also includes AI systems or (smaller) AI applications.

An internationally active consultant for team and personnel development and coaching (Interview 8). Like the previous interviewee, this expert can also look back on many years of experience as an employee in various national and international companies. Based on this know-how, this interviewee provides his expertise as a personnel and team developer to various companies. In most cases, the projects are closely related to new technologies and applications. Thus, the expert can demonstrate extensive experience with the implementation of new technologies and related organizational changes.

**Background Information**

Topics of the expert interviews

The expert interviews were oriented around several thematic complexes. The interviews each followed the same pattern and the same internal order in order to deal with these thematic complexes. The experts were completely free in their answers, so they did not have to follow any selection options or other guidelines. The topics covered were as follows:

(a) Own experience with AI technologies and AI systems in development and application
(b) Technical basics and interrelationships of AI technologies, possibilities of different approaches and applications, limits of different applications and approaches, trends and forecasts of (technical) development paths and innovations in the future
(c) Reliability and trustworthiness of AI based systems and applications in the expert's respective industry or industries.
(d) Importance of ethical rules and other general value specifications for employee orientation in connection with AI systems in the company
(e) Changed task descriptions, role descriptions and responsibilities in the company through the use of AI-based systems
(f) Changes and developments in employee communication and employee management through the use of AI-based systems in the company.

As described, all interview partners have extensive and long-standing knowledge and experience with various possible applications of AI technologies. Overall, all experts agreed that artificial intelligence is leading to more and more processes in companies being automated and made more efficient. Especially in routine work and clearly described processes, this development is already very apparent and will become even more pronounced in the future. All areas and sectors are affected, from manufacturing and traditional industry to activities and professions in the service sector and administration.

- **AI as an "Assistant" in Everyday Working Life**

As a further aspect of the development just described, the experts emphasized that AI systems would increasingly appear as "assistants" in everyday work. These assistant systems would make suggestions or give instructions on what should be done based on calculated probabilities or learned patterns. Here, AI would have a very clear and perceptible effect for the individual in his or her everyday work. The experts were unsure whether this would be received rather positively or negatively by the employees concerned. In the past, several experts reported experiences in both forms. For example, employees had perceived the support provided by assistance systems as beneficial because it had led to time savings in various task areas. Such experiences confirm, for example, the statements of the technology acceptance model, which assumes that people always accept new technologies quickly if they perceive a reduction in their workload. According to the experts, other employees perceived such assistance systems as a restriction on their freedom of decision and felt patronized. This experience is in line with the self-determination theory, according to which too many (clear) guidelines tend to restrict employees' willingness to perform and motivation. This experience could also be explained with the jobs demands-resources model in such a way that the necessary resources were not available to the employees in this case and they would have lost motivation because of this. With the knowledge of which resources are necessary to promote motivation and willingness to perform, these negative experiences could probably have been avoided in practice.

According to the experts, the technical understanding of employees in cooperation with and the applications of complex digital systems and tools is an important factor for acceptance and effectiveness in use. Thus, employees should definitely understand how the systems they use work and also what logic underlies them. The experts disagreed on the degree or depth of technical understanding. While the experts with their own technical and development backgrounds were of the opinion that employees and managers should have a general technical understanding and should focus primarily on operation and application, the interviewees who do not have any explicit technical training or experience emphasized that it is certainly important to provide employees and especially managers with detailed technological knowledge in order to enable them to deal effectively and efficiently with AI-based technologies and to use them in their everyday work. For example, the CEO of the software and systems developer and the managing director of the developer of AI-based financial software said that basic knowledge was important. The CEO of the online marketing company or the consultant for organisational development, for example, were of the opinion that a deeper understanding and detailed knowledge of technical principles and functions were critical for success. A possible, but unverified, explanation for this could be that the experts from the technical business fields tend to consider it advantageous if the AI users only have application knowledge, since the advanced technological detailed knowledge is their own domain and ultimately also their competitive advantage.

#### ■ Changes in Job Profiles

With regard to the changes in job descriptions and job profiles, the experts interviewed were again very unanimous. All of the interviewees predicted that the automation of processes and activities would give employees new freedom. This freedom, which at the same time also represented new and higher demands, would primarily be in the areas of creation, strategy and business development. It can therefore be safely assumed that employees in various professions and activities will have to develop and apply more creativity. "Creative" should not only be understood in a quasi-artistic sense. Rather, it is a matter of employees increasingly having to develop individual solutions for different problems and being able to react more quickly and flexibly to challenges (Interview 1, 2, 5, 7, 8). At the same time, employees have to develop more competence in strategic and long-term thinking and decision-making. If routine and standard work were to be taken over by autonomous and AI-based systems or assistants, the focus of human work would inevitably shift to these dimensions. Both creative and strategic tasks would require employees to be able to think and act simultaneously on two time horizons: Extremely short-term and individual, and equally related to and oriented toward long-term goals. This means being able to scrutinize one's own work and one's own decisions in a more reflective and self-critical manner and to recognize and evaluate interrelationships (Interview 3, 5, 6, 8). These are abilities that AI systems cannot develop at present or in the foreseeable future, but which correspond well to the human and biological way of thinking and deciding. At the latest, this raises the question of responsibility and the assumption of responsibility. In the classical hierarchy of companies, strategic and long-term decisions were reserved for managers at the top and highest levels, and still are in most cases today. Managers and employees in companies must therefore redefine whether and how responsibility must be redistributed and whether employees in AI-conditioned new work profiles are at all ready and willing to take on responsibility.

**Background Information**

The tasks of people

According to the experts, the task of people working with AI systems will be to weigh up, question, classify and assess the results and suggestions of AI systems. This will require technical expertise and industry- or profession-specific competence, as well as a higher degree of independence and personal responsibility. However, it remains to be seen whether and how employees will accept these new and higher demands. While some experts advocated clear guidelines for decision-making and assumption of responsibility on the part of management, other experts did not consider this to be necessary or expedient. Several experts emphasized the importance of ethical principles that had to be anchored in the corporate culture in order to create the conditions for employees to make their own decisions and assume more responsibility. All experts also pointed out that the current legal situation in Germany and Europe was still completely unclear and open at this point.

The increasing importance of knowledge of human nature, emotional intelligence and empathy was emphasized, as it were, by all the experts interviewed. The importance of interpersonal contact and communication will clearly increase through the use of AI systems and tools in the course of the changes described and discussed. This applies both within companies and towards customers and partners.

In some professions and industries, this is more of a minor shift, while in others it can certainly be compared to a paradigm shift. Particularly in sectors and professions that were previously characterised by a very rule-based process of communication and relationships regulated by all kinds of regulations, employees and managers would be faced with major changes (Interview 1, 2, 4, 7, 8).

Overall, the experts interviewed were largely in agreement in their assessments regarding the focus of the forecast developments and changes. These assessments and forecasts also coincide with the findings of science and research from the recent and recent past on the issues and topic areas discussed. There is a consensus in research that with the use of AI systems it will become necessary for employees to take on more responsibility and to constantly develop new tasks and goals for their own "human" activities themselves, because autonomous systems will take over the more or less simple and clearly defined standard tasks in processes and workflows. What has not been clearly researched and defined in this context is the question of how employees themselves evaluate these forecasts and what they expect and consider necessary in order to be able to cope with these new requirements. For this reason, the next step was to conduct a quantitative survey to provide answers to these questions.

# Expectations of Employees Towards "AI Jobs"

Contents




A. Moring, *AI on The Job*,
https://doi.org/10.1007/978-3-662-64005-0_9

Expectations guide our behavior, influence our decisions, and motivate us. For these reasons, people's expectations provide information about which factors and which resources are important and decisive for a successful AI implementation and productive cooperation between people and AI-based systems and applications. For this purpose, the models and theories already presented in the previous chapters are used again. They guarantee a reliable and secure analysis of the results and thus equally reliable derivations and recommendations for the implementation in practice.

## 9.1 Questioning

The structure of the quantitative survey is based on the topics defined in the expert interviews described above. The survey is intended to identify the requirements and expectations of employees in companies with regard to the implementation of and collaboration with AI-based applications and systems. The jobs demands-resources model from economic and psychological research, which was presented in detail earlier, serves as the basis. The model describes the relationship between job demands and resources in relation to the motivation and productivity of employees.



From different disciplines of scientific research and with a variety of theories and models described here before, it is known and proven that in the so-called human-machine interaction, the willingness and acceptance of people towards (new) technical applications are the most important key to success and productivity in application and cooperation.

In other words, the potential of artificial intelligence can only be realized in organizations if the people in the organization are also involved and motivated.

The requirements (demands) on employees in cooperation with AI-based systems were worked out and defined for the following survey in expert interviews as just described. For this purpose, around a dozen experts were interviewed who already have practical experience in the development and use of AI systems in companies in various industries.

Based on these requirements, a catalogue with a total of 15 questions was developed and widely distributed in an online survey via various channels in order to reach a sufficiently large and generally representative, i.e. non-branch-specific, number of respondents. The study was able to collect responses from about 600 ($n$ = 580) respondents. The survey period ran from mid-February to mid-May 2020.

The answers to the questions from the questionnaire thus ultimately define the requirements for the framework conditions and prerequisites ("resources") that enable productive collaboration between employees and AI systems and AI applications in companies.

**Background Information**
Topic areas of the survey.

The questions are based on the same topics that had already been defined for the qualitative expert interviews.

(a) Own experience with AI technologies and AI systems in development and application
(b) Technical basics and interrelationships of AI technologies, possibilities of different approaches and applications, limits of different applications and approaches, trends and forecasts of (technical) development paths and innovations in the future
(c) Reliability and trustworthiness of AI based systems and applications in the expert's respective industry or industries.
(d) Importance of ethical rules and other general value specifications for employee orientation in connection with AI systems in the company
(e) Changed task descriptions, role descriptions and responsibilities in the company through the use of AI-based systems
(f) Changes and developments in employee communication and employee management through the use of AI-based systems in the company.

A total of 15 questions were asked and answer options were given for these questions, in some cases several answer variants were also possible. As described, the questions were derived and formulated from the statements of the expert interviews. In the following, the questionnaire with the possible answers for the interviewees will first be reproduced:

1. Artificial intelligence is leading to more and more processes being automated and made more efficient, especially when it comes to routine work and clearly described procedures.
   - Yes, I have experienced that in my company as well
   - No, this is not (yet) the case in my company
   - Less standard work and monotonous processes are an attractive prospect for the future.
   - same here
   - I don't agree
   - If it doesn't apply in their case, what's the reason?
   - I feel most comfortable in the same and familiar processes
   - I don't know what to do instead…
   - I don't trust machines to do such standardized tasks as well as humans.
2. Due to the development described under 1, AI systems will increasingly appear as assistants in everyday work. These systems make suggestions or give instructions on what should be done based on calculated probabilities or learned patterns.
   - I would not rely on such suggestions
   - that certainly makes my job easier

   What would have to be in place for you to rely on these types of suggestions? (Multiple answers possible).
   - Nothing, such sophisticated machines are yet almost perfect
   - I need to know what information and data the proposals are based on
   - I need to understand how the calculation method behind it works
   - I need to know what the purpose and goal of the proposal should be

3. AI systems are based on complex and complicated fundamentals. Technical understanding is always an aid in the operation and use of technologies. However, in private and professional contexts we also use complex technical devices without explicit technical knowledge.
   - For me, the main thing is that it works. How to do this, I do not need to know
   - For me it is important to fundamentally understand the functioning and the interrelationships in order to work with such systems.
   - For me it is important to really understand the functionality in detail when working with such systems.

   Who do you think is responsible for knowledge transfer (if deemed necessary)?
   - Everybody has to teach himself that
   - This is the task of the company or the responsible managers.
4. The automation of processes and activities creates new freedom for employees. This will primarily be in the areas of creation, strategy and business development.
   - That's a problem for me, because I don't know anything about that…
   - This is positive for me, because I always wanted to take care of it more intensively.

9

5. The task of humans in collaboration with AI systems will be to weigh, question, classify and judge the results and suggestions of AI systems.
   - No problem, I'm up for it
   - I don't see how that's going to work.

   If you still see difficulties here, what is the reason? (Multiple answers possible).
   - I lack the technical understanding of how AI systems work
   - I lack a classification on how far I am allowed to go in my judgement and decision making
   - I lack a clear definition of how far I am allowed to deviate from the suggestions of the AI system.
   - I lack a clear authority to also decide against the suggestions of the AI system, if I consider that useful
   - I lack clear ethical rules for assessing AI results and proposals.

   Who do you see as responsible for providing the possible missing information and rules described above (multiple answers possible).
   - The legislator
   - The management of the company
   - The responsible executives in the upper and middle management
6. Knowledge of human nature and emotional intelligence as well as empathy are particularly important competences for the requirements described under 5.
   - That's already the case in my job today, I don't see any difference.
   - These skills are still too little appreciated and used today

   What do you think are the necessary framework conditions so that people skills, empathy and emotional intelligence are taken seriously as important competencies in connection with AI in the company? (Multiple answers possible).

- A clear corporate mission
- A corresponding corporate culture
- Clear ethical business rules
- Managers who (exemplify) these competencies

7. From the previous topics, it is clear that with the use of artificial intelligence it will become necessary for employees to take on more responsibility and to constantly develop new tasks and goals for their own "human" activities themselves, because autonomous systems will take over the more or less simple and clearly defined "standard tasks". Is this a positive prospect for them or a negative one?
   - I'm looking forward to it
   - I do not find this attractive

   Regardless of the previous answer: What would you need in order to take more responsibility for your activities and decisions? (Multiple answers possible).
   - A clear corporate mission
   - A corresponding corporate culture
   - Clear ethical business rules
   - A clear hierarchy and chain of responsibility in the company
   - Managers who guarantee their employees freedom and responsibility
   - A clear job description for my job
   - A clear boundary where and how far AI systems are allowed to decide and implement themselves in the company
   - sufficient technical training in AI applications
   - In-depth programming knowledge for AI systems and applications
   - Opportunities to experiment with AI systems
   - technical equipment (hard- and software) up to date

## 9.2 Results

After the explanation and presentation of the questions and the questionnaire, the results will now be presented and evaluated.

One third of the respondents state (◘ Fig. 9.1) that they already have practical experience with AI and its effects on work and processes. Accordingly, two-thirds of the respondents have not yet had any contact with AI technologies and applications in their own day-to-day work.

According to their own statements, the majority of respondents would like to be freed from routine work (◘ Fig. 9.2). Artificial intelligence is viewed positively by just under 90% of respondents in this context. This result may initially be surprising in its clarity. However, the result confirms the statements of the technology acceptance model as well as the self determination theory, according to which an easing of work through technology and less standard and routine work is considered attractive by people in principle.

Most of the respondents who rated the future scenarios described as negative stated that they feel most comfortable in unchanging and familiar processes, followed by the uncertainty of not knowing what to do after routines have been dis-

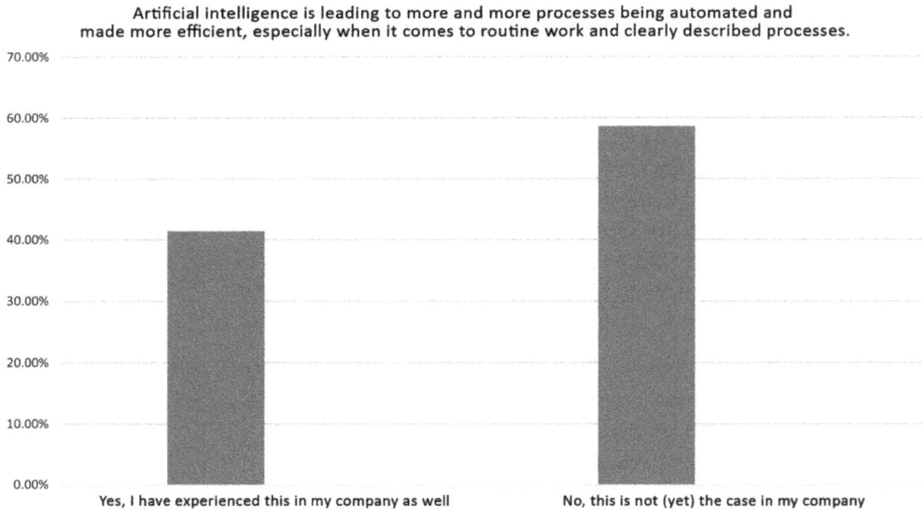


**Fig. 9.1** Survey

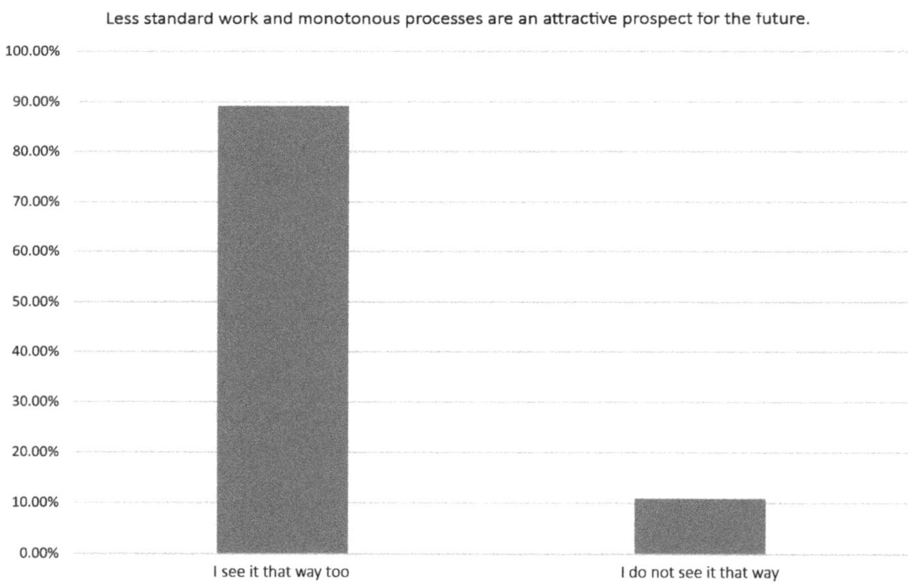


**Fig. 9.2** Survey

continued (Fig. 9.3). Clear and unambiguous structures generally give people a sense of security in their everyday working lives. If the structures and hierarchies change as a result of the use of AI and new cuts in jobs and organization, this means a special challenge for these people.

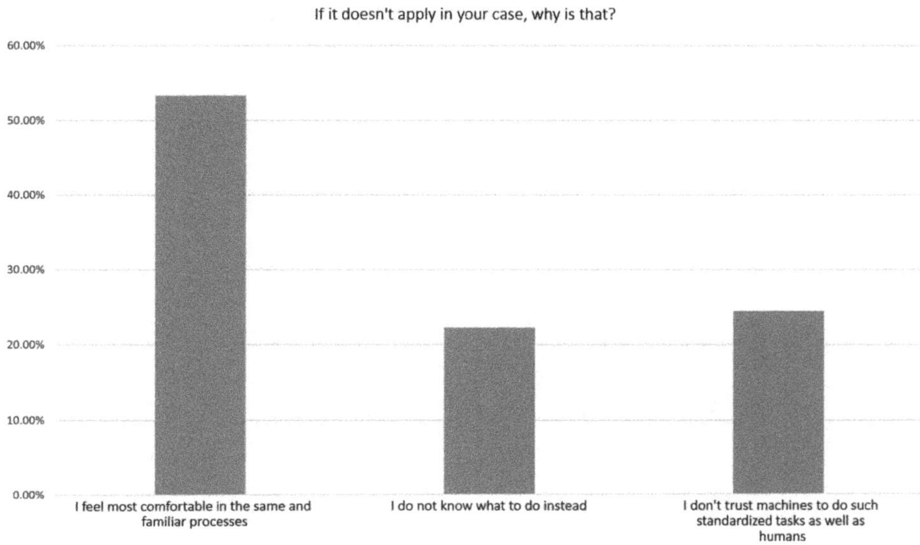


**Fig. 9.3** Survey

With regard to the cooperation with AI-based assistance systems or intelligent agents, the respondents reflect different assessments and evaluations (Fig. 9.4). Around one third of respondents doubt the trustworthiness of AI predictions. Two-thirds of the respondents consider the (expected) facilitation of their own activities to be more important and significant than possible miscalculations of the AI systems and are willing to trust the assistants.

When asked about the prerequisites for trusting and productive collaboration with AI assistance systems, more than 80% of respondents stated that they needed to know what information and data the system's suggestions were based on (Fig. 9.5). More than 70% of the respondents stated that they needed to know what the purpose and goal of the respective suggestion should be. Around half of the respondents stated that they needed to understand how the respective technical calculation method behind or in the assistance system worked, which produced the suggestions. These statements allow the analysis that whoever wants to increase the acceptance of AI systems among employees must make it transparent to them from which data the forecasts come and what the (programmed) goal of the forecast or optimization is. In some cases, the goal of AI or machine learning applications is clear: always when it comes to so-called "supervised learning". The descriptions of this have been given in the chapter on Artificial Intelligence technologies. In other cases of so-called "unsupervised learning", however, the goal is merely specified in general terms (e.g. cost optimization or minimization of runtimes), but cannot necessarily be named or described in concrete terms. Likewise, as described in the corresponding chapter, there are applications that search for their goal themselves and "learn" and optimize exploratively. It is therefore difficult or even impossible to make the goals of AI use transparent to employees ex ante.

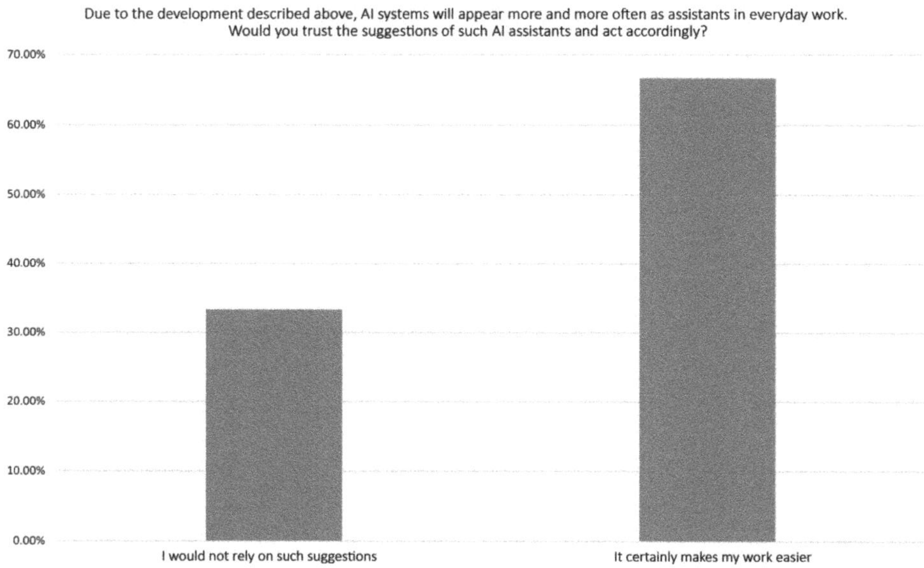




■ **Fig. 9.4** Survey

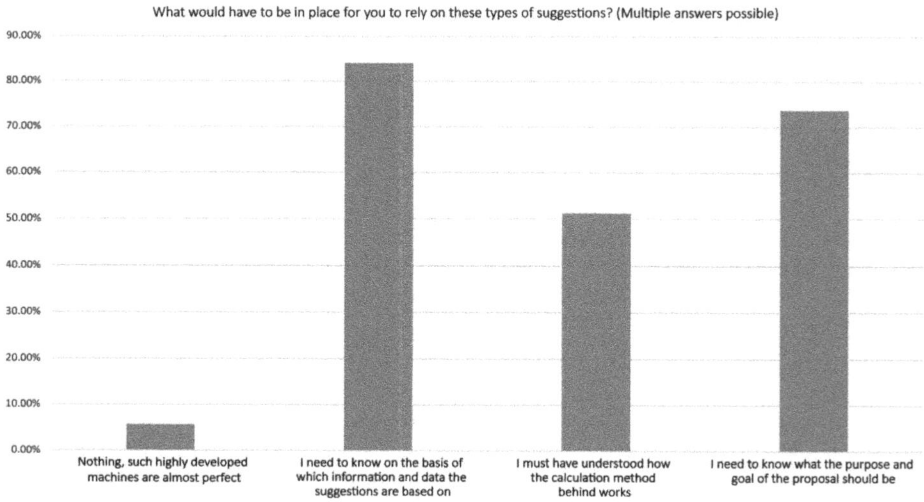


■ **Fig. 9.5** Survey

In addition to an understanding of the respective goal, the respondents also appear to need a technical understanding (■ Fig. 9.6). Around three quarters of all respondents state that it is important for them to have a basic understanding of the functionality and interrelationships in order to be able to work with AI systems. One in ten of the respondents state that they really need to understand the functionality in detail in order to work with such systems. For around 15%, reliable

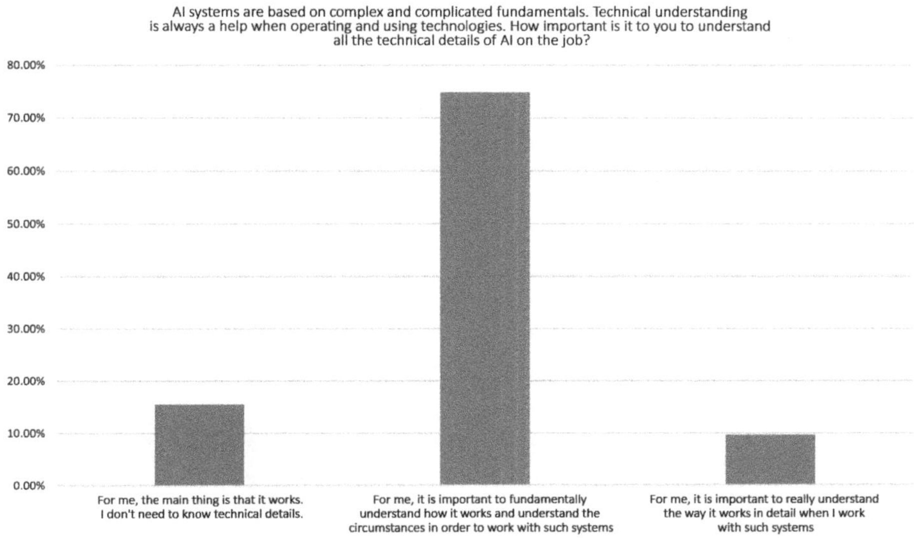


**Fig. 9.6** Survey

functionality alone is decisive and a technical understanding, on the other hand, is not. This result is in line with the assessment of the surveyed experts from technically oriented companies and markets, who, as described, were of the opinion that a basic technical understanding of AI-based applications is sufficient for productive human-AI interaction. Nevertheless, the clear majority of respondents are concerned with concrete information and further training, not just instruction in the respective user interface, so that respondents are prepared to really cooperate and work productively with the corresponding system.

When it comes to imparting the knowledge considered necessary by the respondents, the vast majority expect knowledge to be imparted by the management level of their own company (Fig. 9.7). There is no significant willingness on the part of the respondents to undertake their own further training. The reason for this is that AI applications are clearly related to the professional context and optimized for this purpose.

With regard to new freedom for creative and strategic tasks through the use of AI-based systems, the opinion and the expectations of the respondents are very clear (Fig. 9.8). Nine out of ten respondents describe these prospects as positive, because they wanted to deal with such tasks more intensively anyway. This sounds very positive at first, but it also poses challenges and dangers. There is a potential danger here for company management and executives to underestimate the challenges of change and transformation. The impression can arise that the implementation of AI and the changes in the company will “go through on their own”, so to speak, because “everyone is looking forward to it”. However, there is no innovation and change process that would take shape on its own. The initially quite positive statement therefore means a great challenge. The expectations of employees are very high. However, before implementing AI technologies, every company must

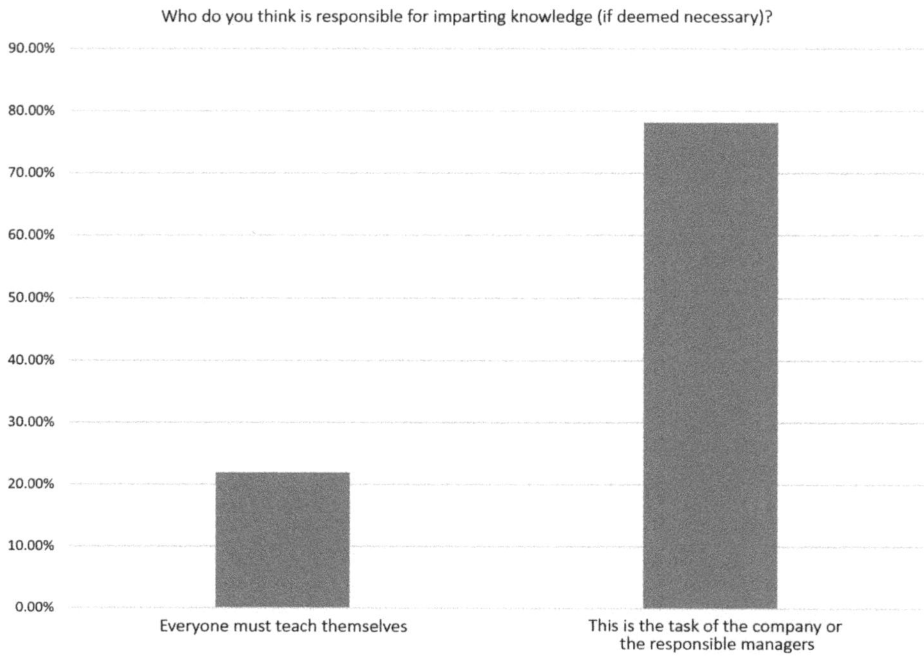


9

**Fig. 9.7** Survey

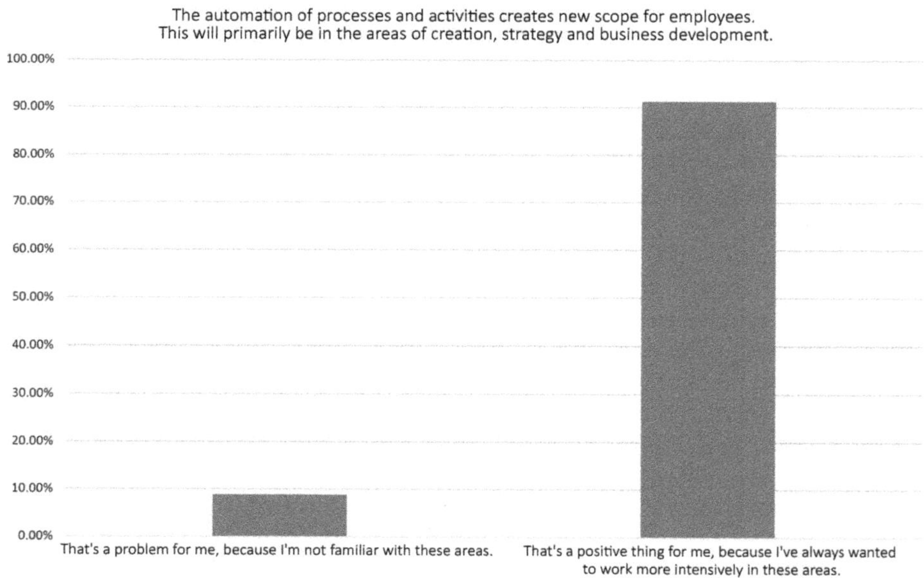


**Fig. 9.8** Survey

ask itself: What are the specific jobs and tasks with a new strategic, creative and developmental profile? In the vast majority of cases and companies, this has probably not even been defined yet!

In the course of the changes discussed in the previous questions and answers, the scenario arises that the task of people working with AI systems will be to weigh up, question, classify and assess the results and proposals of AI systems (◘ Fig. 9.9). Nearly 90% of respondents said they are confident in their ability to critically question AI systems and judge their outcomes. At the same time, however, most of the same respondents previously said that they would first have to be able to understand the basics of AI systems in the first place and that the company would have to teach them this. So, interestingly, these statements basically don't match up. The respondents seem to have a tendency to overestimate their own abilities in dealing with AI and autonomous systems.

Asked more deeply, the respondents nevertheless give several reasons that make it difficult for them to assess the results and recommendations of AI assistance systems (◘ Fig. 9.10). Apparently, when asked to reflect, respondents become aware that there may well be challenges for them in their new work role interacting and cooperating with AI. First and foremost, the respondents want clear ethical rules to judge AI predictions and AI based specifications. Likewise, they expect permission to disregard the system when it seems appropriate to them, i.e. to continue to be "masters of the process". Respondents seem to be aware that they are inferior to AI systems in their specific performance (calculations, statistics,

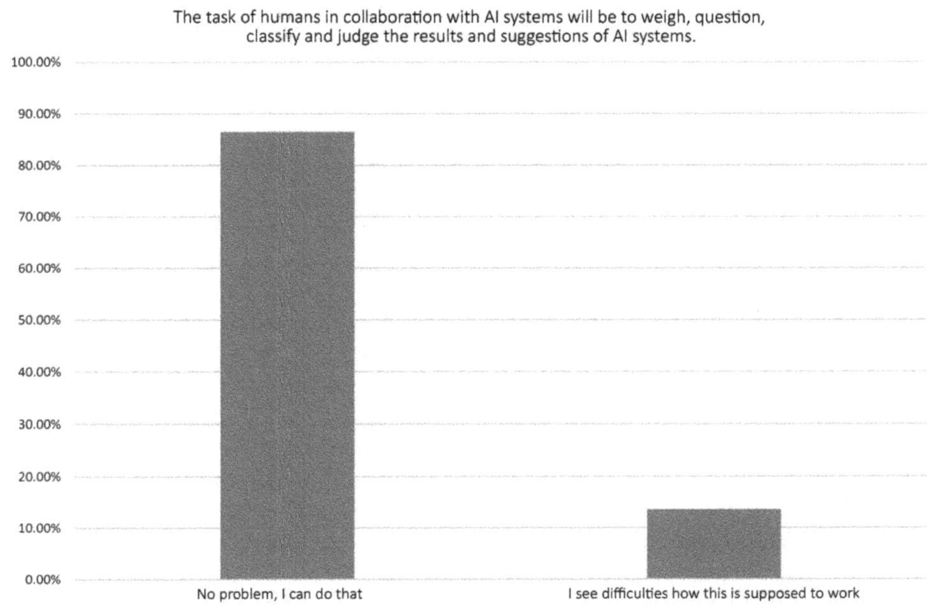


**◘ Fig. 9.9** Survey

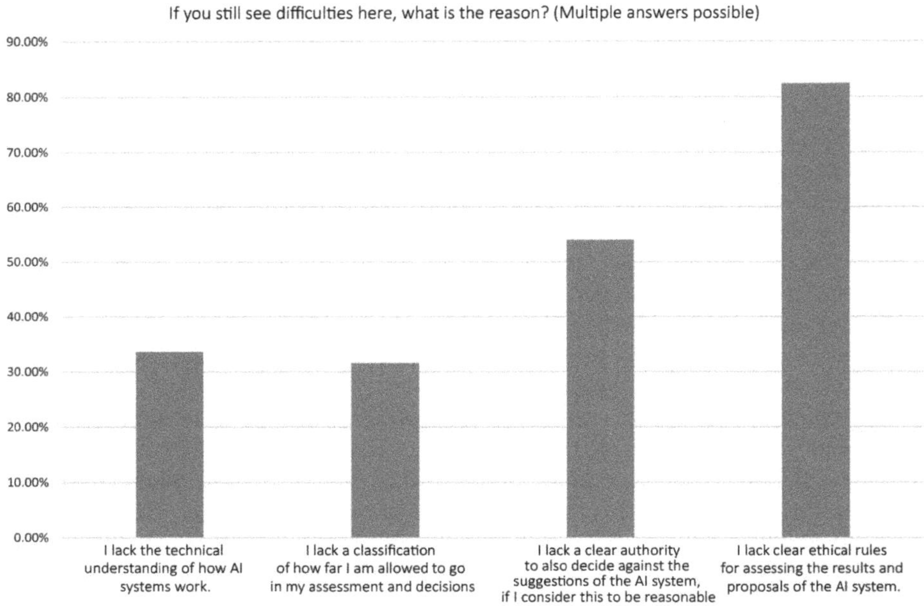


9

**Fig. 9.10** Survey

optimization). Therefore, other rules and domains – in this case the domain of ethics and the backing of superiors – seem necessary for them to legitimize the claim to control the processes in cooperation with AI systems. In most companies, however, it can be assumed that such ethical rules for cooperation with AI systems have not even been defined yet. In addition, the question arises in companies and in individual, concrete AI applications whether it makes sense at all to always give employees permission to "overrule" the AI. In many cases, this could counteract the goal and purpose of AI use, for example, when AI systems are used to optimize processes and costs, and this optimization would then in turn be counteracted by human "overruling" to varying degrees. Here it becomes clear that in many places with the implementation of AI systems, a new design of jobs according to the criteria "fully autonomous" and "human decision" is necessary, because otherwise the necessary acceptance on the part of the employees is likely to be lacking and a human-machine/system cooperation would not function as hoped.

The respondents have a clear attitude to this and a clear expectation as to who is responsible for formulating the rules and information called out in the previous answer (Fig. 9.11). According to the respondents, the management, the board of directors and likewise middle management should define the necessary rules and thus ultimately assume responsibility. In this context, two fundamental questions arise: (1) Are corporate executives able and willing to assume this corporate and equally moral responsibility? (2) do the executives in companies themselves have sufficient detailed technical understanding and functional knowledge of the AI systems used that they would be in a position to formulate such ethical rules and to

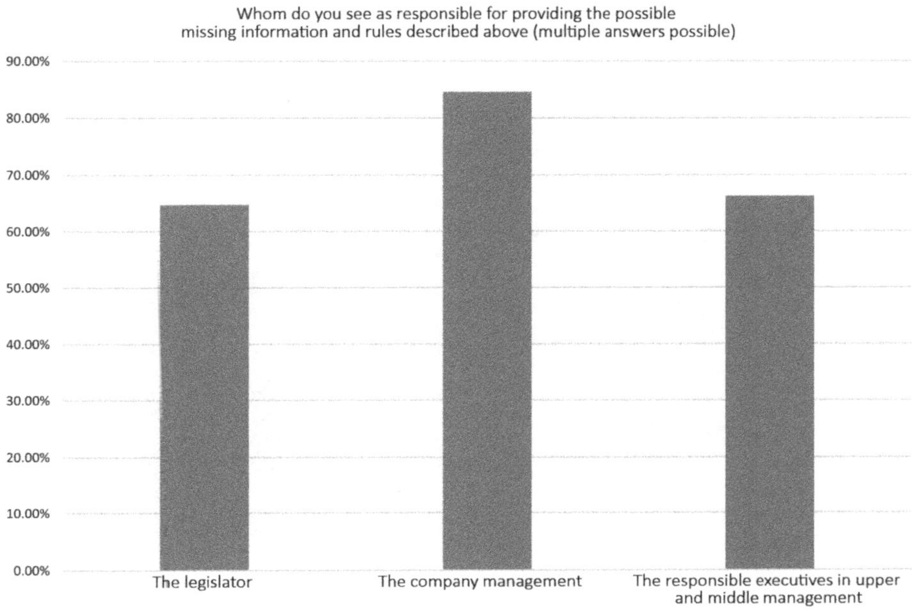


**Fig. 9.11** Survey

draw binding and sufficiently well-founded boundaries for the decision-making areas of autonomous systems and employees? This point would again speak in favor of the opinion expressed in the expert interviews, according to which managers must have a profound and detailed understanding of AI technologies in order to achieve productive human-AI cooperation, because otherwise they are not in a position to fulfill the above-mentioned expectations of their employees.

Another clear statement made by the experts in the qualitative explorative interviews was that knowledge of human nature and emotional intelligence as well as empathy were particularly important competencies for the changes and requirements with and in human-AI cooperation (Fig. 9.12). Around 60% of respondents believe they have more emotional and social requirements in their job, as this would merely be an increase in the proportion of these, not generically new requirements. However, just under 40% of respondents also say that these aspects do not currently play a sufficiently important role in their job.

When asked about the necessary framework conditions so that knowledge of human nature, empathy and emotional intelligence are taken seriously as important competencies in connection with AI in the company, the respondents state several conditions of almost equal importance (Fig. 9.13). Around 85% of respondents cite managers who exemplify these competencies as an important framework condition or resource that they require. 80% of respondents also mention a corresponding corporate culture as important. Around 65% of respondents are in favour of clear ethical corporate rules. A clear corporate mission statement is important for around 30%. This means that respondents want to see social and

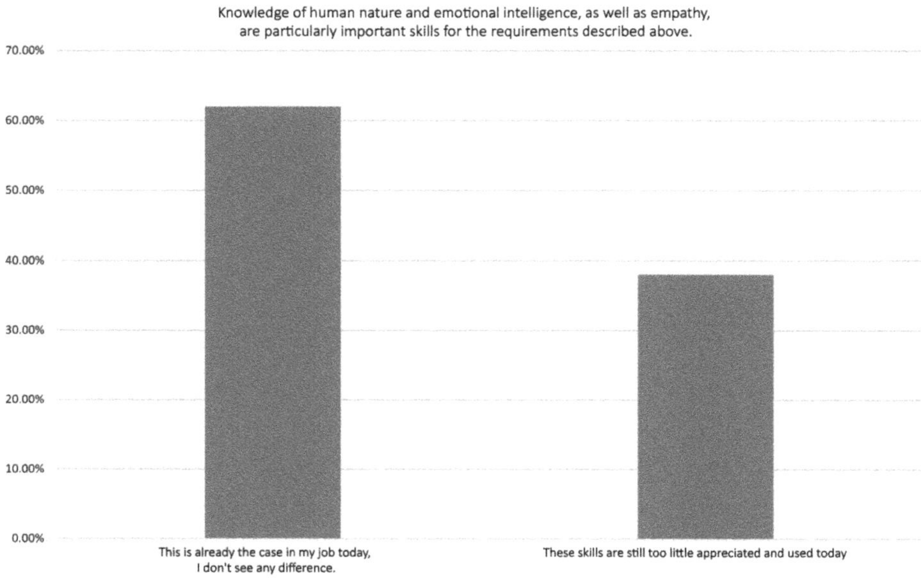


9

**Fig. 9.12** Survey

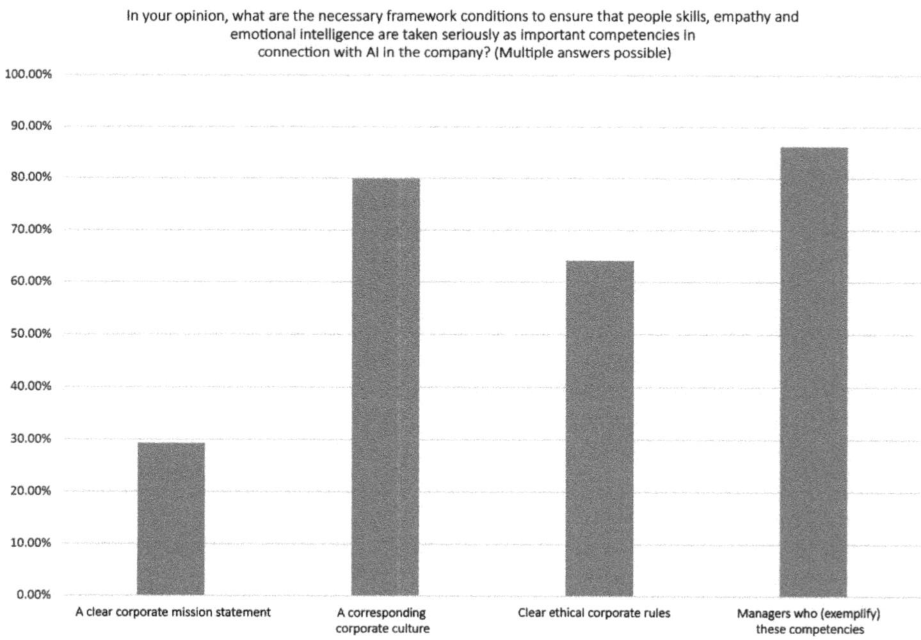


**Fig. 9.13** Survey

emotional intelligence and competence exemplified by managers. This is a manifestation of a change in expectations with regard to the understanding of management and communication. Particularly through the use of highly technical and complex AI applications, the need for more empathy and human interaction with each other is obviously increasing among employees. This also applies to communication, which, according to the expectations of employees, should also become more emotionally intelligent and empathetic. Managers are thus faced with the challenge of finding a new way of dual communication with the increasing implementation of artificial intelligence: The communication with and control of more or less autonomous machines and systems and the communication and motivation of employees who also want to act more and more autonomously. This is made even more difficult by the fact that employees expect and demand more autonomy and freedom – but they would rather delegate responsibility to managers and have an ethical set of rules on which they can base their decisions when cooperating with AI systems.

In their clear majority, however, the respondents state that they are willing to take on responsibility and also set their own goals in their own work (◘ Fig. 9.14). Around 90% state that they are happy to take on more responsibility and to keep developing new tasks and goals themselves. Conversely, this is not an attractive prospect for one in ten.

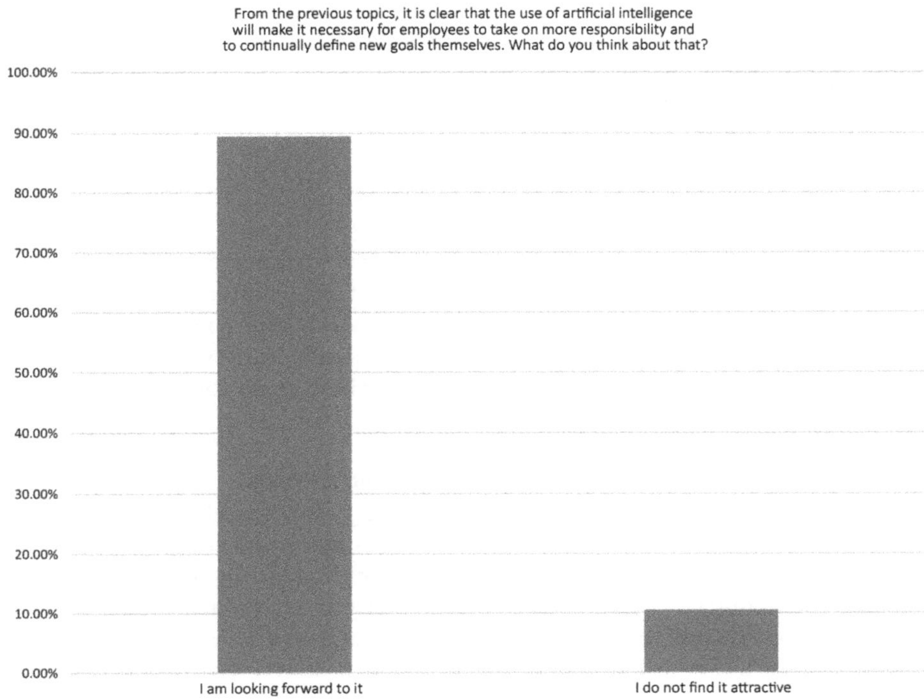


◘ **Fig. 9.14** Survey

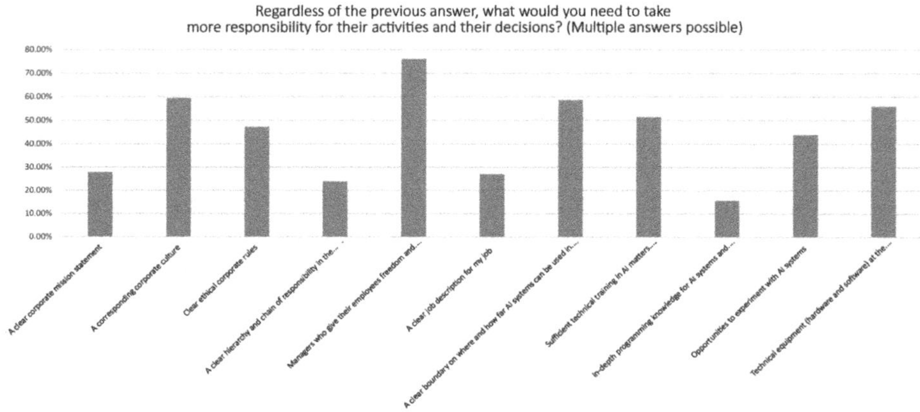


**Fig. 9.15** Survey

The respondents prioritize quite clearly the most important prerequisites for being able and willing to take on the freedom and responsibility that is assessed as fundamentally attractive through AI use (Fig. 9.15). Three quarters of respondents state that managers who guarantee their employees the freedom represent the most important prerequisite in their eyes. 60% see a corresponding corporate culture as an important prerequisite. Likewise, just under 60% of respondents identify a clear boundary as to where and to what extent AI is used as an important prerequisite for successful human-AI cooperation and the assumption of responsibility. This is followed by sufficient technical equipment and adequate technical training as important framework conditions.

## 9.3 Analysis of the Results

The following analysis examines the significance of the quantitative survey results in relation to the jobs demands-resources model and in relation to the technology acceptance model. This analysis is intended to provide answers to the question: What needs to be done for productive and effective human-AI collaboration to succeed?

### Analysis According to the Jobs Demands-Resources Model

As described at the beginning of this paper, the jobs demands-resources model deals with so-called "stressors". These are circumstances and conditions in everyday working life that represent challenges or even burdens for the person(s) concerned. The changes brought about by the implementation of Artificial Intelligence in an organization and the resulting changes in processes and requirements can be clearly defined as such stressors. According to the jobs demands-resources model, employees in such situations place increased value on maintaining and, if possible, even accumulating their resources for performance in their daily work. This postulate of the jobs demands-resources model can be considered as confirmed by the empirical survey of this thesis. The majority of the interviewed participants stated that they would be relieved in their work by artificial intelligence – i.e. that they would save their resources – and also formulated claims for an expansion of their autonomy and a debt to be discharged by the company when it comes to acquiring the necessary knowledge for dealing with new AI technologies – i.e. an accumulation of existing and new resources. Various results of structural equation modeling analyses in the jobs-demands-resources model show, as described in the corresponding chapter in this book, that personal resources are not sufficient to balance the relationship between job demands and exhaustion. This means, therefore, that in the opinion of the employees, the respective company has an obligation to contribute its own part to a "sufficient" resource endowment. This result is also reflected in the expectations formulated in the survey that the company should provide further training for AI use and should shape the circumstances of the work in such a way that employees feel well provided for and motivated in their resource endowment.

**Background Information**

Resources for high employee motivation

So what are these circumstances and resources that ensure high employee motivation in connection with AI implementation and AI use, which is characterized by specific workplace features. According to the interviewees, the most important resources are "managers who guarantee their employees freedom" and an "appropriate corporate culture" that focuses on autonomy and self-determination of the individual. This is followed as other important resources by "clear limits on where and to what extent AI is allowed to make its own decisions" and "clear ethical corporate rules" for dealing with AI-based results, forecasts or specifications. Only then do the resources "sufficient technical training" and "technical equipment" follow. It is noteworthy here that with a very complex technology and new technical applications, it is not the technical resources or technical know-how that ranks first among the important resources, but it is interpersonal, communication and social resources that have the most important influence on openness, willingness to perform and motivation. However, this result supports the previous foundations of the jobs demands-resources model, according to which social support is generally the most important buffer against stressors.

The other buffers of the jobs demands-resources model are also confirmed in the survey:

- The extent to which the onset of a stressor is predictable (e.g., role clarity and performance feedback).
- To what extent the reasons for the presence of a stressor are comprehensible (e.g. through information from superiors or institutions).
- The extent to which aspects of the stressor can be controlled by the individual and whether that individual can experience it (e.g., work autonomy).

The majority of respondents stated that role clarity between humans and AI is very important to them (clear boundaries and ethical rules), as is open communication from managers and a corresponding corporate culture, and also their own experienced work autonomy (guaranteed freedom).

Communication between employees, and especially between employees and managers, therefore plays a decisive role here as a resource for employee motivation. This is also confirmed by the results of the survey in this work with regard to the implementation and application of AI-based systems and tools. Two poles of the new leadership culture are emerging, which at first glance do not seem to be compatible with each other – and which present managers with entirely new tasks and challenges. The extent of this development has only been analyzed by a few authors and scientists. However, they are all largely unanimous in their prediction that the leaders of the future are likely to accept and "lead" a new kind of employee – i.e. AI machines or autonomous robots – into their organizations. As the capabilities of AI machines increase and provide opportunities for new products, business models and information use, the workplace of the future will change, as robots will be able to perform human-like tasks. Because of this, leaders will no longer lead humans alone, but humans and machines will (have to) join forces in achieving their goals, creating a whole new dynamic within companies.

The implication is that communication standards in AI programming should be set to address both humans and machines. Therefore, leadership and AI management are interconnected. However, a clear connection of machine leadership or machine management is currently impossible. The reason: machine leadership is currently not about leadership, but about setting rules, processes and monitoring them. For managers and executives, however, the following still applies: even if machines do not yet possess emotional intelligence, the manager must monitor the AI program, decide on critical tasks and make the best possible use of resources. Therefore, the role of a manager in the future is characterized by understanding how initially specific AI solutions with a low threshold of use can help to take over and automate processes and work steps. This means that two different requirements are involved here at the same time. Namely, clear rules and control on the machine side and empathy and ownership and freedom on the human side of leadership. Uniting and reconciling these two poles of leadership philosophy is the greatest challenge in the transition to the AI era for companies and for the people who lead these companies.



**Tip**

So how should executives go about facing and overcoming this challenge? With the wide variety of use cases and technological possibilities that AI now offers, one of the biggest challenges for executives is screening for adequate use cases and analyzing the associated risks for their companies. Even though AI can automate almost everything, it is still obvious that not every problem should be solved by AI, because sometimes other rule-based options are more viable. Consequently, executives need specific knowledge of the technology to understand the components involved in an AI project. A solid understanding of what is happening in a project is critical and must be evaluated with the necessary technical know-how and understanding as background.

For executives, it is precisely the specific and high-performance characteristics that make AI so scary and yet fascinating. Top management is often already striving to integrate AI into organizations, although middle management still wants to put the brakes on or even hinder this process, as they perceive AI projects to be very technical and complex and apparently simply feel overwhelmed in many cases with the specific skills required in mathematics, data science and IT in practice. As a result, experts and practitioners largely agree that leaders in Germany need to start making the change and working on their skills as soon as possible. The same applies to the development and motivation of employees who are expected to use AI systems. After all, it has long been known that intrinsically motivated employees ultimately perform better – this remains unchanged in the AI age. For this, a helpful theoretical model for implementing AI in organizations and motivating employees can be Tidd and Bessant's (2013) innovation management framework, as it places innovation management at the heart of the organization and allows leaders to work towards innovation at different levels, starting at the incremental level to achieve more creative and radical innovation over time. Their model is appropriate for addressing the implementation of AI solutions and capturing the value of innovation, which is often missing in many other models and frameworks. In addition, their model reflects the learning elements of Scouller's (2011) model with an iterative process of acquiring knowledge and experience that leads to the adoption of successful innovations.

So it is not only technical skills and structures that are crucial, but also the development of one's own emotional intelligence is essential for a manager. Because the upcoming changes directly affect the employees. For this, it is crucial that the manager truly understands their perspective, that of the employees. In addition, there is the indispensable technical understanding, in turn, of AI systems. So when it comes to AI, we are faced with a new dual leadership philosophy that must bring two different requirements into productive harmony: Clear technical rules and control in the management of autonomous systems and, at the same time, empathy and creativity in dealing with and managing people.

In addition, there is another requirement that is linked to the described resource of social support and corresponding communication and culture, which was also clearly defined as crucial in the empirical survey and confirms the buffer or motivational effect of the jobs-demands-resources model: Ethical rules and boundaries in and for human-AI cooperation. For the interviewees, such rules represent an important orientation, especially when it comes to the conditions under which employees may act and decide against the results and specifications of AI-based systems. Here, companies and managers are faced with a very important task. Namely, to define ethical rules of conduct and decision-making in human-AI cooperation for themselves and their employees. Companies and managers should not "shirk" this task, because it is a crucial resource for employee motivation in the implementation of cooperation with artificial intelligence. This task should not be underestimated in its importance and scope, as it is not only about procedural rules for the own employees in the job, but also about general social and societal standards, which become important and have an effect beyond the current job and the current employment. This takes corporate governance and corporate social responsibility of companies and organizations to a new level. The formulation and living of appropriate ethical rules and values inevitably changes an existing corporate culture or even triggers a longer-term and profound cultural change. This is of course a major challenge; at the same time, however, the survey showed that a corporate culture that matches the ethical rules and values is an important resource for employees and a great motivator for a day-to-day working life shaped by artificial intelligence.

Every company and every organisation is of course obliged to define these rules and values for itself and its own needs and circumstances. However, there are already well-suited orientation aids and working bases for this. These include, on the one hand, the "Criteria for Human-Machine Interaction in AI" of the Learning Systems Platform (◘ Fig. 9.16) presented earlier. Arranged according to four clusters, they provide basic key points that should be used.

Furthermore, companies and organisations should refer to the "Ethics Guidelines for trustworthy AI" of the High Level Expert Group of the European Commission. The guidelines define prerequisites and requirements for so-called "lawful AI", for so-called "ethical AI" and in the third stage so-called "trustworthy AI". The Guidelines distinguish once again between ethical and trustworthy in the quality of AI applications, with trustworthy being classified above ethical. This is also understandable. "Ethical AI" can be regarded as a prerequisite for general acceptance by employees of an organization; AI that is even trusted by humans, on the other hand, can be regarded as the basis for (possibly exponentially) productive collaboration between humans and artificial intelligence.



A concrete concept for the development of ethical rules and principles for the use of artificial intelligence and assistive systems is the so-called MEESTAR model. MEESTAR stands for "Model for the Ethical Evaluation of Socio-Technical Arrangements" (Manzeschke 2015). The core of the model is a workshop in which participants from companies, organizations or project groups come to a common, well-founded ethical judgment that has consequences for their decisions regarding the design, communication and operation of a technical assistance system. In the MEESTAR model (◘ Fig. 9.17), Manzeschke describes the identification and evaluation of ethical problems from three different perspectives: (1)

| **Cluster 1: Protection of the individual** | **Cluster 2: Trustworthiness** |
|---|---|
| ■ Safety and health protection<br>■ Data protection and responsible performance recording<br>■ Sensitivity to diversity and freedom from discrimination | ■ Quality of available data<br>■ Transparency, explicability, and consistency<br>■ Responsibility, liability, and system trust |
| **Cluster 3: Reasonable division of labor** | **Cluster 4: Supportive working conditions** |
| ■ Adequacy, relief, and support.<br>■ Responsibility for action and situational control<br>■ Adaptability, fault tolerance and individualizability | ■ Spaces for action and rich work.<br>■ Conduciveness to learning and experience<br>■ Communication, cooperation and social inclusion |

◘ **Fig. 9.16** Source: Huchler, N. et al.: Criteria for human-machine interaction in AI. Approaches for human-centred design in the world of work, Plattform Lernende Systeme, Munich 2020

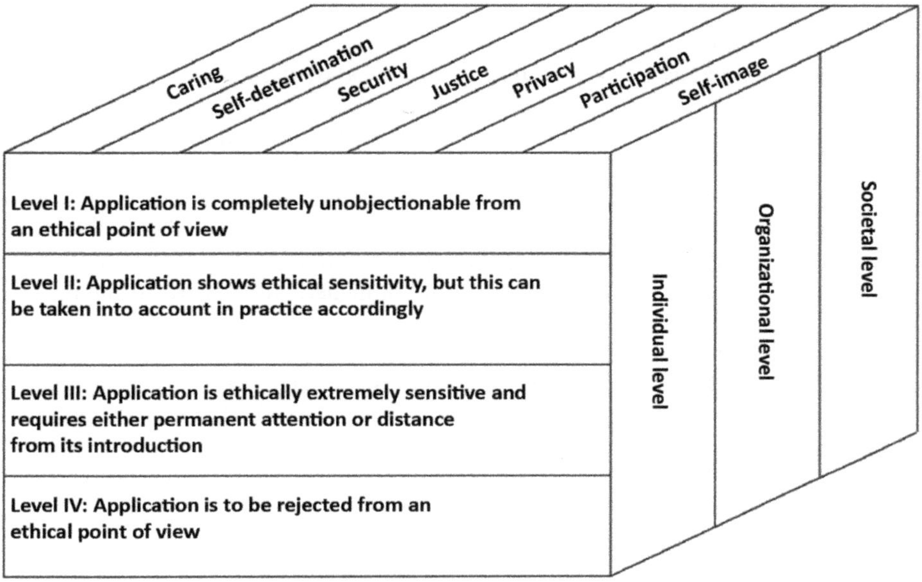


**Fig. 9.17** Source: Manzeschke (2015)

individual, (2) organisational and (3) societal. On the individual level, very different perspectives are imaginable, but mostly the perspective imagined is that of the potential user of the assistance system. On the organisational level, it is also possible to imagine many different organisations involved in the development, dissemination and maintenance of the assistance system. Here, too, a focus usually dictates concentration on the organization that will later offer the assistance system to be developed. On the societal level, it is a matter of taking a generalizing view. What does the introduction and dissemination of this technology mean if it is used across the board, if it becomes a standard for dealing with the specific problem described, if it is combined and extended with other technologies?

The results of the empirical survey also support the resource maintenance theory associated with the jobs-demands-resources model. This assumes, as described earlier, that work resources have a particular effect on motivation or work effort when job demands are high. According to the "conservation of resources" (COR) theory, people seek to preserve, conserve, and protect what they value, for example, various material, social, personal, or energetic resources. In the context of artificial intelligence, the resource of personal autonomy and decision-making authority based on ethical rules can be considered particularly worthy of preservation.

#### ■ Analysis According to the Technology Acceptance Model

In addition to the jobs demands-resources model, the technology acceptance model has also been presented in ▶ Chap. 4. This model defines various so-called acceptance variables. The TAM consists of the acceptance variables "perceived usefulness" (PU), "perceived ease of use" (PEOU), "attitude towards using" (ATT), "intention to use" (ITU) and "actual use of the system" (AUS). These variables are related to the assumption that a positive attitude towards a (new) technology also leads to an intended use. This postulate is supported by the empirical survey of this study, because the majority of respondents stated that they had a fundamentally positive attitude towards AI applications and that they wanted to use them in their everyday work or were already using them to some extent (around two-thirds of respondents had no experience with AI systems and applications, while almost 40% of respondents had). The technology acceptance model also describes a correlation between a technology's perceived positive effect and its actual productive use. This correlation can also be considered confirmed with regard to the respondents of the empirical survey. In most companies and in most organizations, however, AI systems are still a rarity. In this respect, in further AI implementation and use, it is important to ensure that a corresponding positive effect manifests itself as quickly and clearly as possible for the employees concerned, so that human-AI cooperation succeeds. The so-called "items" of the TAM can serve as a kind of checklist for this:

- quality of work
- control over work
- work more quickly
- critical to my job
- increase productivity
- job performance
- accomplish more work
- effectiveness
- makes job easier
- useful



These items are remarkably consistent in their message and content with the expectations of employees, which respondents indicated as important resources according to the jobs demands-resources model: Control and decision-making authority, higher performance, and relief from burdensome standard tasks in favor of creative and strategic tasks.

#### ▪ Analysis According to the Self Determination Theory

An analysis of the results of the qualitative and quantitative findings of this thesis against the background of the self determination theory presented at the beginning and the three basic motives of motivation can provide some insights into why very specific resources in the job are seen as so important for productive human-AI collaboration. However, it should be noted here that these analyses cannot claim any (work) psychological depth either, as the author lacks the necessary scientific expertise in this regard. From the point of view of general (change) management and personnel management, however, they appear to be entirely justifiable and appropriate.

For example, self determination theory emphasizes a strong connection between a distinct and unambiguous corporate culture and the motivation of employees in that company. Similarly, the self determination theory emphasizes the importance of a positively perceived social environment characterized by trust for high motivation among employees in companies and other organizations. Both of these relationships can be clearly confirmed by the surveys in this study. Respondents cited a clear corporate culture with ethical rules for human-AI collaboration and trusting communication with managers and a guarantee of safety on the part of managers in the event of any decisions against AI specifications as the most important factors for motivation in the use of AI-based systems. The results of this study confirm the statements of the self determination theory, according to which the individual experience of autonomy, of perceived competence and the experience of being integrated provide motivation for employees, or demotivation arises if these experiences are denied or remain. This is also in line with the statements of the qualitative and quantitative surveys of this thesis, which also defined precisely these three aspects as the most important in relation to cooperation with artificial intelligence systems and applications.

**Analysis According to the Basic Principles of Performance, Connection, Power**

With regard to the three basic principles of motivation, a clear insight can also be formulated as to which aspects play a motivational role when it comes to using and collaborating with AI-based systems and applications.

Performance motivation is defined as the pursuit of excellence, of surpassing oneself, of proving oneself to others, and of enjoying or experiencing the task-related activity itself. AI as a support for human work should in principle increase precisely these aspects of motivation, as it makes people potentially more efficient in their experience and also in fact.

Connection motivation is defined as integration into a group and the experience of commonalities. If employees can experience such commonalities in cooperation with AI systems, for example by the AI being able to respond to the individual and his habits and current constitution, then this will promote motivation. Connection motivation also arises, as described at the beginning, from a perceived sympathy in cooperation with others. In connection with machines and technologies, sympathy can also be equated with user-friendliness and usability. It is therefore important to design AI systems and applications that are as intuitive and easy to understand as possible. This is not too simple a requirement against the background of the technological complexities described in ▶ Chap. 3. These findings are also consistent with the statements of the technology acceptance model. Connection motivation can also arise from fear of rejection. This means that people's motivation is affected when they are rejected in various forms.

> This in turn means that AI systems and applications should be designed and deployed in such a way that situations of human failure vis-à-vis AI and situations of conflict with AI should be avoided. The ethical rules, which have been presented more extensively before and which are considered necessary, can serve precisely to avoid such conflicts between humans and artificial intelligence.

The power motivation is defined as satisfaction through the influence on others. In relation to autonomous systems and artificial intelligence that works and acts more or less independently, this is an important aspect. Power motivation is also described as a feeling of strength and the experience of self-efficacy. Here there are the already described connections and overlaps with the self determination theory.

> The results of this work also come to the clear conclusion that it is precisely this feeling of self-efficacy that is rated as particularly important for motivation in collaboration with AI.

The interviewees also want to be able to decide against the specifications of the AI in case of doubt, they want to be able to rely on ethical rules as an authority above the AI and they want to strengthen creative and strategic tasks in their activity, i.e. they want to be able to influence the development of their environment. Giving power to AI-based systems is only easy when it comes to repetitive, burdensome and boring tasks. On the other hand, it is difficult when it comes to acceptance and trust in AI-based systems. Here, respondents indicate that they need a technical understanding of how AI works and transparency about the data used and the goal of the AI application. In addition, respondents indicate that they want to overrule the AI when in doubt and have the confidence to do so, which is clearly related to the important feeling of self-efficacy and influence or power. This phenomenon especially towards advanced technical systems is already known under the name of "algorithm aversion" (Dietvorst et al. 2014). People are clearly less fault-tolerant towards technologies than towards humans and fundamentally trust the results of technologies and systems less than the results or opinions of other people. Even when the technologies and systems objectively and evidenced produce better results than humans. So solution to this algorithm aversion is proposed to give the humans in the collaboration, with the technology or the system a small margin (in the single-digit percentage range) to adjust the result or the suggestion of the system (Dietvorst et al. 2015). This is also confirmed by the findings of this research, as respondents reported higher acceptance and motivation to engage in AI collaboration when they can influence the outcomes and specifications of the AI and claim their own ethically based domains of decision-making power over the technology. Power motivation theory also speaks of "resource superiority" as a prerequisite for a sense of power and strength. This is consistent with the assumptions and propositions of the jobs demands-resources model, which have already been discussed and analysed in detail, and the associated aspects of resource conservation and resource accumulation. The investigations of this thesis now make it possible to also precisely name and justify at which concrete points and with which concrete resources this superiority must be given so that a productive and effective human-AI collaboration can succeed.



**Key Factor Trust**

In summary, it can be clearly defined after these considerations that the leadership of tomorrow, in view of the identified framework conditions and requirements, requires above all trust towards the employees and the AI systems in equal measure. It depends on an open, creative mindset on the part of everyone involved, as well as entrepreneurial thinking at all levels and, last but not least, the will to constantly learn and develop. That's why an innovative culture in an organization that starts with a small, supportive solution and gradually evolves the company to more accomplishments is the appropriate approach for leadership to begin the transition to AI in the enterprise. An understanding of the value of "intrapreneurship" in the organization is essential for this.

## Literature

Dietvorst, Berkeley J.; Simmons, Joseph P.; Massey, Cade: Algorithm Aversion. People erroneously avoid algorithms after seeing them err, Journal of Experimental Psychology, 10/2014

Dietvorst, Berkeley J.; Simmons, Joseph P.; Massey, Cade: Overcoming Algorithm Aversion. People will use algorithms if they can (even slightly) modify them, Philadelphia 2015

Manzeschke, Arne: MEESTAR. Ein Modell angewandter Ethik im Bereich assistiver Technologien, in: Weber, Karsten; Frommeld, Deborah; Manzeschke, Arne; Fangerau, Heiner (Hrsg.): Technisierung des Alltags. Beitrag für ein gutes Leben?, Stuttgart 2015

Scouller, J.: The three levels of leadership: How to develop your leadership presence, knowhow and skill. Kemble, Gloucestershire 2011

Tidd, J., & Bessant, J. R.: Managing innovation: Integrating technological, market and organisational change (Fifth edition). Chichester 2013

# 10 Guide for Practical AI Implementation

Contents




A. Moring, *AI on The Job*,
https://doi.org/10.1007/978-3-662-64005-0_10

There are clear criteria and factors for the successful implementation of AI and its use in companies. These have been worked out in the previous chapters. Now it is a matter of the concrete procedure for implementation and the associated decision-making process. This chapter describes these points and presents useful tools and procedures.

In the previous chapter, we answered the question "What needs to be done for productive and effective human-AI collaboration to succeed?" from several perspectives. This also answers the question of which resources have the greatest impact so that employees are willing and able to engage in such productive collaboration. See also the note at the beginning of ► Chap. 8.

> The question that follows is therefore: What should a guideline for the implementation of AI in organisations look like in the light of the analyses and findings of this study?

It is important to remember that the responsibility for a successful approach lies with the company or the executives. On the one hand, this results from the logic of the matter: The company management is precisely there to lead the company and this also includes changes, innovations and implementations. In addition, the survey of this study has shown that there is a high expectation on the part of the employees towards their own companies to fulfil this duty. Why this is so, we can easily deduce with the knowledge of the jobs demands-resources model: People need their own resources and, above all, resources provided by the company in order to be able to fulfil the (changed) demands of their job.



As we have already seen in ► Chap. 5, we must assume that a resource gain in itself has only a modest effect and acquires its real significance in connection with the (actual or possible) loss of resources. This means that labour resources unfold their motivational potential especially when workers are confronted with high work demands. The introduction of new systems and technologies without prior experience in the organization or on an individual level, such as AI systems, may well be understood and categorized as such a high work demand. At the same time, this is also associated with a loss of tasks and resources. Namely, tasks that an AI is supposed to take over from humans because it can perform them better and resources that are lost because with the loss of the task, the previous resources necessary for it are (no longer have to be) provided.

**Tip**

Guide in three steps

The most important resources according to the results of this research's own survey are first and foremost managers who guarantee freedom and the existence of defined boundaries and ethical rules for AI in the company. A guide for implementation should be guided by the following three steps in the given order:

1. Where and for what purpose AI? – At which points in your own processes and workflows should AI be used? Which tasks and work steps should AI take over? For what clearly defined purpose should AI be used?
2. What results should the AI produce? – Is the use of AI expected to reduce the workload of employees? What does this relief look like? Will the use of AI lead to more freedom and freedom of action? What do these freedoms consist of? How should the freedom be used?
3. What ethical rules apply? – What are the company's ethical principles for the use of AI in general? What are the company's ethical principles for the use of AI specifically in the tasks and areas defined under point 1?

### ▪ Realization of the AI Implementation

Before answers to the questions in the three areas listed above can be jointly developed and defined, there must be sufficient technical understanding, at least among the people involved. This means that technical training is unavoidable. This also coincides with the expectations of those interviewed for this research, who clearly defined such knowledge transfer as an important resource for successful AI cooperation. The expectation of technical training and transparency in the functioning of AI systems were described in detail in ▶ Chap. 8 as a prerequisite for employee cooperation with these new systems. Moreover, without this knowledge, the first step of implementation cannot even be realized: The definition of where and for what purpose AI is to be used.

To do this, it is first necessary to make the processes and tasks in one's own organization clear and transparent for everyone. Technologies determine processes and organizations. Most of the time, we think it's the other way around – or at least that's what we tell ourselves. According to the motto: a new technology should optimize processes, reduce costs and thus secure margins. Everything else should remain as it is. But that is not the case. Various studies show the effect of companies using digital technologies to ultimately reshape decision-making incentive systems, information flows, hiring practices, and other aspects of their management and organizational processes. This also means that as companies adopt or transition to new technologies, they not only increase their productivity quite significantly, but also simultaneously increase the need for skilled employees and decrease the need for unskilled employees. "Skilled" here refers to the general qualification of employees in terms of expertise, independence, creativity and economic thinking, as well as the ability to deal specifically with the new technologies. This is also the case with regard to "artificial intelligence".

In general, it can be roughly stated that for every dollar or euro invested in new digital technologies, another ten dollars or euros are subsequently invested in "organizational capital" or in further training, new hires or the redesign of business processes. Restructuring often eliminates a lot of routine work. What remains are tasks that require disproportionately more judgement, competence and corresponding previous training. The companies that invest the most in new digital technologies also tend to make the biggest organizational changes, usually with up to 7 years' lead time before full performance improvements are realized. Such companies also experience the greatest increase in demand for skilled workers. This further supports the need for technical training and education, as well as the need for co-creation, as this is the only way to practice and build decision-making and management skills. The time lag is due to the fact that supervisors as well as employees first have to find new applications for the new technologies – i.e. find and define the "where" and "what for". This is because a technology that is acquired for a specific purpose usually has many other possible applications in the medium and long term, for example by combining it with other technologies or machines, by transferring it to other processes, by adopting applications from other industries, etc., and so on. Computers were once acquired to automate computing operations (cf. Bresnahan et al. 2001; Brynjolfson et al. 2002; Fitoussi et al. 2004). But what are computers used for today?! The Internet was once implemented to send electronic mail. What is the network used for today?! Even with Artificial Intelligence, the subsequent applications in enterprises are huge compared to the limited applications we use today. So in enterprises, the introduction of new technologies is not about optimizing existing processes through technology, that is, merely repaving the well-worn paths, so to speak, to make it easier and more convenient. It's about thinking about how a company could (possibly) be redesigned from the ground up to properly leverage new technologies and realize the full potential of performance improvement. Creativity and the transformation of organizations determine the success of investments in digital technologies.



So the best way to use new technologies is not to simply use a machine or an algorithm for human work in the future, but to restructure the processes. This means that some employees are no longer needed in the places where they previously worked. At the same time, however, there will be a need in the company in other places. Probably at positions in the new processes and the new organization and with new competence profiles that did not exist before. For these reasons, it usually takes time before such changes are actually implemented and new technologies introduced after they have been invented. At the same time, however, the speed of external competition and also of internal processes is increasing precisely because of these new technologies. It is a matter of technical (basic) understanding of the new possibilities and modes of operation of "artificial intelligence", it is a matter of authentic and credible leadership in the necessary change processes described – incidentally an exclusively human quality that no machine can provide – and it is a matter of promoting and developing one's own employees in and with the organization.

Companies must therefore ask themselves the question "Where and for what purpose can I use artificial intelligence in my company?" And rightly so, because AI will change a great deal in companies and perhaps even overturn what we still regard as normal and self-evident today. The use of AI must always be adapted to the individual company. But there are a few basic rules that are valuable for orientation.

**Tip**

What does AI do best?

First of all, it helps to be clear once again what artificial intelligence actually is at its core and what AI does best. It is optimizations and predictions. Both based on complex calculations, which in the end all have the goal of minimizing uncertainties as much as possible. Exactly how this is done and where the differences, the strengths and weaknesses of the various systems and approaches lie has been described in detail in ► Chap. 3 of this book. Precisely because it is indispensable in order to get a good deal closer to the answer to the question "Where and for what purpose can I use artificial intelligence at all in my company?"

The common practice of implementing Artificial Intelligence in various forms and various technologies and manifestations is to develop AI tools. The important thing in developing such AI tools is not to focus on the existing "job" that needs to be done. That's why AI won't destroy jobs en masse, precisely because the technology can't take over jobs. It's also not about specific occupations or even strategies of work and production. It is about functions or tasks. Functions or tasks are basically a collection of decisions. Decisions are based on predictions and evaluations, and these in turn are fed by information or data. Decisions within particular functions and tasks always share these characteristics in a very similar way. This is the character of the functions or tasks. Differences then exist in the type of action and execution that follows from the decision.

1. So the first and most important task when deciding on the use of artificial intelligence in companies is to first get a clear overview of the functions and tasks in one's own company.
2. The next step is to analyze and describe exactly how and where these functions are embedded in existing workflows and which jobs belong to them or are involved.
3. Next, the individual functions and tasks must be analyzed to determine what kind of decisions are made where and how in these functions. This is the starting point for the implementation of AI technologies, because – as described above – it is about predictions and evaluations.
4. When it comes to predictions and probability or scenario calculations, AI technologies are unbeatable.
5. The situation is not so clear-cut when it comes to the respective valuations. Here, each company must decide whether the evaluation of a prediction should also be left to technology or whether human evaluation and judgment is necessary here. At this point, the ethical rules to be worked out later play a decisive role.
6. When it comes to unique classifications and categorizations, AI technologies are already very good today and can work autonomously.
7. When it comes to evaluating and assessing contexts and various influences, or creatively processing information and developments, this can only be done by human skill and experience.

This in particular shows the importance and significance of cooperation between people and technology. Only those who do the work for themselves and their company to seriously and conscientiously proceed according to the pattern described above will also be able to leverage the full potential of artificial intelligence for productivity and competitiveness. Two effects are possible here. First, AI can completely take over certain tasks and functions, taking them out of the existing workflows of the humans in the company. That in itself is a major challenge, because it redefines those workflows and, inevitably, the tasks, responsibilities, accountabilities, and hierarchies in the company. Second, AI can also create entirely new tasks and functions and, as it were, bring them into the existing or even new workflows. And this also has consequences for tasks, responsibilities, accountabilities and hierarchies in the company.

Of course, the whole thing is an extensive and complex work for all involved. But it also has other positive effects, besides the ones mentioned above. With technical understanding and a clear definition of where and for what AI-based systems should be used, a positive basic attitude will most likely emerge. Understanding and a sense of controllability tends to make people feel positive about a challenge. And according to the technology acceptance model, this positive attitude then also leads to the use of new technologies.

The following step of the implementation consists of defining results. Basically, we can also call this step "expectation management". It is about clearly stating which freedoms will result from the changed processes and procedures that have been defined in the first step. This part is simple. At the same time, however, it is also a matter of defining which responsibilities will result from the changed processes and procedures. This step is not easy. One hurdle is that employees or managers may not want to relinquish responsibility. At the same time, another hurdle is that employees would like to have more freedom but do not want to take on responsibility, as the survey in this study has shown. So here we are dealing with a classic negotiation process of change management. In case of doubt, the responsibility must always lie with the person who has the technical understanding of the AI application and understands and can classify functionalities and backgrounds. In addition, the findings on algorithm aversion described in the last chapter can also be used here. Opening up room for manoeuvre in the use of AI-based results and recommendations for people makes it easier for them to cooperate with the technology and also to take responsibility.



Based on the results of the first two stages of implementation described above, the last stage can now be started. This involves the definition of ethical rules for human-AI cooperation. For this purpose, for example, the recommendations of the EU Expert Group already described in the previous chapter can be taken as a basis, or other sources mentioned in the previous chapter. The corporate values and the corporate philosophy are also foundations and at the same time sources of inspiration that should be used. The MEESTAR model, which was also presented, can also be used here. The elaboration of ethical rules and boundaries thus unfolds other important effects for the implementation besides the actual goal. Open and trusting communication, which we know from the self determination theory to be important and powerful, can have an effect even before the actual AI implementation. The joint development of ethical rules has an effect on the basic motives of security, power and control and promotes a positive attitude and thus also an openness to the use of and collaboration with AI-based systems. The inclusion of people in the entire implementation process and the fact that the defined ethical rules apply to everyone – whether human or machine – also has positive effects on the motivation to connect and thus also on the open-mindedness and self-confidence towards AI-based systems in implementation and use.

Another model for human-AI interaction based on the MEESTAR model just described is the reflection and evaluation tool HAI-MMI – humanizing AI men-machine-interaction by Huchler (2020). It is based on the premise that not imitation and outdoing humans should be the driving forces for technology development, but the search for a higher-value complementary relationship between humans and technology. The best results can also be expected from this. Evidence of disproportionate increases in productivity and effectiveness with human-AI cooperation understood and realized in this way has been presented and analyzed in several places in this book. The model incorporates the three dimensions of human-machine interaction quality, levels, and design criteria. On this basis, existing AI solutions in companies and organizations can be classified into five different classes, from poor to medium to high quality of human-AI interaction. The evaluation is based on the criteria of coordination, division of labor, learning, adaptivity and empowerment. The HAI-MMI model concentrates on the design, functionality and operation of the AI solution itself; other influencing factors such as the organizational design or the culture in the company or the respective management and communication are not included (◘ Fig. 10.1). For a qualified and comprehensive

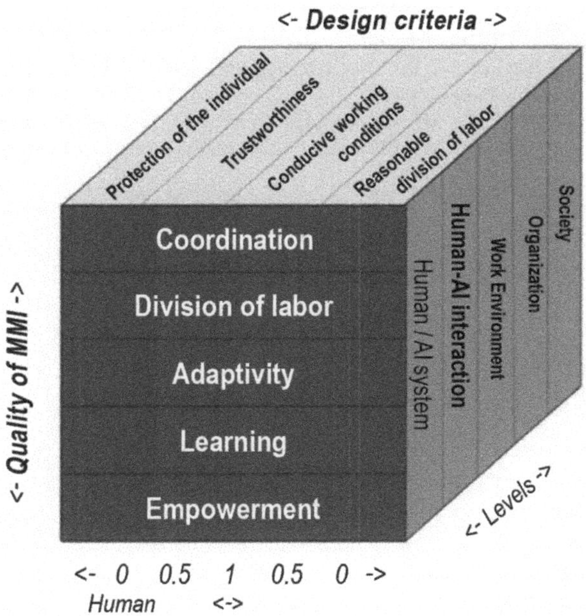


◘ **Fig. 10.1** Source: Huchler (2020)

evaluation and classification of possible AI solutions before the decision and implementation, the evaluation tool provides valuable services in any case.

In implementation, the buffer effect already described for the jobs demands-resources model can be used through performance feedback. Constructive feedback not only helps employees do their jobs more effectively, but also improves communication between supervisors and employees. When specific and accurate information is provided in a constructive manner, it leads to both employees and supervisors improving or adapting and changing their performance to meet new challenges. Appreciating employees for good performance helps keep them motivated and signals them to continue in that direction. Since everyone is in a learning process when dealing with AI-based systems, this should also be easier to do than in established workflows and processes. It is important that positive effects manifest themselves as quickly as possible for everyone involved. Therefore, the implementation should always start with small applications and scenarios for AI use. In the medium and long term, this is the best way to grow and establish a so-called "trustworthy AI" in one's own organization, which can then form the basis for productive collaboration between humans and artificial intelligence – possibly even exponentially.

## Literature



Bresnahan, T.F.; Brynjolfson, E.; Hitt, L.: Information Technology, Workplace Organization and the demand for skilled labour: Firm level Evidence, in: Quarterly Journal of Economics 117/2001, S. 339–376

Brynjolfson, E.; Hitt, L.; Yang, S.: Intangible Assets: Computer and organizational capital, Brookings Papers on economic activity, 2002, S.137–198

Fitoussi, D.; Hitt, L.; Brynjolfson, E.: The IT Iceberg: Measuring the tangible and intangible computing assets, Working Paper 2004

Huchler, Norbert (2020): „Die Mensch-Maschine-Interaktion bei KI in der Arbeit „menschengerecht" gestalten? Das HAI-MMI Konzept und die Idee der Komplementarität." In: DIGITALE WELT 2020

# Supplementary Information




A. Moring, *AI on The Job*,
https://doi.org/10.1007/978-3-662-64005-0

# Index

## F



## G



## H



## I



## J



## L



## M

GPSR Compliance
The European Union's (EU) General Product Safety Regulation (GPSR) is a set of rules that requires consumer products to be safe and our obligations to ensure this.

If you have any concerns about our products, you can contact us on

ProductSafety@springernature.com

In case Publisher is established outside the EU, the EU authorized representative is:

Springer Nature Customer Service Center GmbH
Europaplatz 3
69115 Heidelberg, Germany

www.ingramcontent.com/pod-product-compliance
Ingram Content Group UK Ltd.
Pitfield, Milton Keynes, MK11 3LW, UK
UKHW022003040925
462611UK00005B/531
*9783662640043*